"This is a much needed book to understand technicalities and sensitivities of methodology in diversity and inclusion research. It will be useful for research scholars and practitioners alike in theorising, identifying, collecting, and analysing relevant empirical evidence to develop a nuanced and contextual understanding of diversity."

Jawad Syed, PhD, Academic FCIPD, Professor of Organisational Behaviour and Leadership, Suleman Dawood School of Business, Lahore University of Management Sciences, Pakistan

"It is truly wonderful to see this handbook that is specifically aimed at gender, race, indigeneity, identity, and diversity (GRIID) research as a field of inquiry. Professors Kazeroony and du Plessis have thoughtfully crafted a roadmap to help researchers critically think, plan, and undertake work in this field. The book closes with some personal experiences, thoughtful advice, and future research topics shared by established scholars in the field. This title is a critical resource for doctoral students, faculty, and scholarly practitioners."

Eddy Ng, Professor and FC Manning Chair in Economics and Business, Dalhousie University, Canada

T0372564

DIVERSITY AND INCLUSION

Aimed at assisting doctoral candidates and early-career researchers and their supervisors globally, this book is the first of its type to address the challenges faced by students when proposing new programs of research in the disciplines of gender, race, identity, indigeneity, and diversity within management and business. The problems researchers face derive from a lack of familiarity with the needed alignment of the methodology, conceptual framework, and the nature of epistemologies used in creating a coherent proposal. This results in project delays and unnecessary time in review as doctoral students and committees attempt to provide the required alignment.

Essential reading for students and faculty engaged in these fields of study, the book provides a practical guide on how to navigate through these challenges and to arrive at a workable proposal that meets the requirements of the academy. To assist doctoral students in conducting their research, the book provides narratives that illustrate the complexities of researching gender, race, identity, indigeneity, and diversity in broad terms. It explains the importance of such research in creating positive social change and helping students identify the appropriate conceptual framework, align the problem statement with a purpose, construct the research question and the nature of the study, and identify the correct method to conduct the research.

An essential guide for students and doctoral researchers, this book explains the dominant and marginalized epistemological orientations to acquaint doctoral researchers with the effects of their selections on the outcomes of their research. It provides guidance as to the appropriateness of quantitative or qualitative methods based on the selected epistemology and the problem statement.

Hamid H. Kazeroony has taught in a variety of executive and international programs and is currently a contributing faculty at Walden University, PhD Management Program and is a Professor at Minnesota State Colleges and Universities. He has published widely on issues relating to management education, research methods, and responsible management.

Yvonne du Plessis is a Professor at North West University, South Africa. She specializes in managing organizational behaviour, people and behavioural perspectives in project management, and culture and leadership in multiple cultural settings.

DIVERSITY AND INCLUSION

A Research Proposal Framework

Hamid H. Kazeroony and Yvonne du Plessis

Routledge
Taylor & Francis Group

LONDON AND NEW YORK

First published 2019
by Routledge
2 Park Square, Milton Park, Abingdon, Oxon OX14 4RN

and by Routledge
52 Vanderbilt Avenue, New York, NY 10017

Routledge is an imprint of the Taylor & Francis Group, an informa business

British Library Cataloguing in Publication Data
A catalogue record for this book is available from the British Library

Library of Congress Cataloging-in-Publication Data
A catalog record has been requested for this book

ISBN: 978-0-367-14941-3 (hbk)
ISBN: 978-0-367-14942-0 (pbk)
ISBN: 978-0-429-05403-7 (ebk)

Typeset in Bembo
by Taylor & Francis Books

CONTENTS

ILLUSTRATIONS

Figure

Tables

ACKNOWLEDGEMENTS

We wish to thank the following gracious colleagues whose dialogue, suggestions, and support made this undertaking possible: Stella Nkomo, Jawad Syed, Edwina Pio, Isabel Metz, Thomas Köllen, and Beverly Dawn Metcalfe.

The inputs of experienced researchers—Stella Nkomo, Jenny Hoobler, Juliet Thondhlana, Eddy Ng, and Rana Haq—have contributed to the way forward and possible new areas of research in the field of GRIID.

PREFACE

The globalization of economies, immigration, and gender awareness bring forth a need for linking gender, race, indigeneity, identity, and diversity (GRIID) to corporate social responsibility. The need for developing quality research projects that align with changing expectations with respect to equity rather than simply equality has motivated us to write this book. We will examine the GRIID not as a hierarchical topology but with a view as to construct intersectionality within *Diversity and Inclusion: A Research Proposal Framework*. This book develops a systematic research framework for diversity and inclusion. It further intends to provide support to researchers in the diversity and inclusion domain to conceptualize, identify relevant empirical evidence, interpret data, and examine topics with an intersectional perspective.

Diversity and inclusion are the narratives of our self-perceptions and immediate perceptions of others at the point of contact without reflexivity or reflections. We are labeled as different while attempting to assimilate into an ongoing narrative that others wish us to represent. Within this context, others imagine us with an existential individual identity different from them, and hence attempt to include us in the narrative of their realities. However, when attempting to frame research on explaining diversity and inclusion, the focus should be on the dichotomy of self-perceptions and perception of others based on gender, race, identity, and indigeneity within various epistemes and ontologies as dictated by the etic and emic conditions.

Therefore, as researchers, we found it appropriate to share, within the diversity milieu, the emic and etic conditions of our identities that explain why we are writing this book. As researchers, like others, through heuristic self-examination we realize our identities, understand the inequities and inequalities imposed on us, and find our space with the diverse identities. Writing this book helped us re-examine how we can help doctoral researchers to self-examine their identities to become more objective as they attempt to uncover new meaning or test theories within the frame of diversity and inclusion.

Yvonne's and Hamid's background reflect the emic and etic nature of self-perception and perceptions of others of us. **Yvonne** was born in Namibia (then Southwest Africa as part of the Republic of South Africa) from parents with different nationalities and religions: a German, Catholic mother who could not speak the traditional White native language Afrikaans, and an enlightened Afrikaner father who was brought up in a Dutch-reformed dogma but who became disillusioned about the practice of his religion because of the evils of Apartheid and post–World War II politics that he had to endure. Therefore, she grew up in a multilingual and Church-free home. She was taught that respect for self and others and to ensure dignity are primary human values that should be lived. As she grew up, she did not experience or understand exclusion or discrimination until going to school. Then she had to answer to questions such as "What is your home language?" But they spoke Afrikaans, German, and English in her home. "What is your religion and what church do you go to?" If you did not belong to a specific Church or speak Afrikaans, you were labeled as not part of the in-group. "Why does your mother not attend school meetings in the mornings?" She did not speak good Afrikaans and had a business to run during working hours. Yvonne was also often outcast because she spoke up when Apartheid was practiced but did not understand the meaning of inclusion and exclusion—just that she was different. As a woman who excelled in mathematics and science at school (another oddity in the early 1970s, as science was for men and not women), she went to a university far from home and eventually landed a job where she was the only woman among men. She had to learn to survive and keep her woman identity. Inequality in human resource management practices, such as discrimination in remuneration (30% less than male counterparts) and no housing loans (only available to men as they are the "breadwinners"), made her conscious of discrimination and that some are more equal than others. Having had to adjust, compromise, and accept that people are different in certain aspects as well as similar in others became her live credo . . . Always respect the differences and try to understand how it can affect your relationship with others—not being disrespectful and undignified. Understand your emotion when GRIID confronts you.

Hamid was born in Iran, where his great-grandfather spent half of his wealth fighting the British colonialists around the Bushir by the Persian Gulf. His grandfather was sent into exile before his mother was born, and he was forced to migrate to the United States after the overthrow of the Shah due to the Carter administration's dislike of kings. Over 40 years of his life have been spent in the United States as a foreigner despite his U.S. citizenship. In his early days in the United States, Hamid was harassed constantly because he was Iranian and everyone perceived him as another Iranian responsible for the American hostages in Tehran. As Hamid found his way into corporate America, he faced covert and sometimes overt subtle discrimination as soon as people saw his name or heard him speak with a different accent. Hamid was neither Black nor White, and he was not Spanish or a part of any other recognized minority. Therefore, many safeguards in place were inadequate to safeguard him against discrimination. He felt like an American walking among other Americans, but with a fear like Winston in Orwell's *1984* after making a trip to the Ministry of Truth.

The audience

Both doctoral students and researchers are experiencing a common struggle when proposing new research that addresses gender, race, identity, indigeneity, and diversity across disciplines. This international struggle arises from a lack of familiarity with the needed alignment of the methodology, conceptual framework, and the nature of epistemologies used in creating a coherent research proposal. Often, project delays and unwarranted review time occur with the doctoral students and their committees when attempting to create the required alignment. This book will provide a guide on how to navigate through the common struggles to arrive at a workable research proposal.

The format

This book is not designed to show acceptance or rejection of any theory, theoretical foundation or conceptual framework, or method; it is designed to help researchers examine the feasibility of each, given the guidelines, to find their own path through the process for researching gender, race, identity, and indigeneity in organizations. To help doctoral students and researchers conduct their work, we will provide examples that illustrate the complexities of researching gender, race, identity, indigeneity, and diversity in broad terms. We will explain the importance of such research in contributing to and creating positive social change. We will offer help for students identifying appropriate theoretical and conceptual frameworks, aligning the problem statement with a purpose to provide a unique contribution, research question, purpose, nature of the study, appropriate research design, and methods selected to conduct the research. We will also provide a set of guidelines as a lens for observing research ethics that protect the integrity of the research and of human rights of the subjects. Within this framework, we will explain the importance of understanding and the use of epistemological and ontological approaches to examining topics that can and will support the students' research proposal.

We will explain the dominant and marginalized epistemological orientations to acquaint doctoral students and researchers with the effects of their selections on the outcomes of their research. We will provide guidance as to the appropriateness of quantitative or qualitative methods based on the selected epistemology and the problem statement.

This book aims to serve doctoral and researchers who are conducting studies in GRIID within various disciplines and will be engaged in collecting and interpreting data. We aim to draw attention to peculiarities of conducting GRIID research, explaining the impact of selected methods and adopted theoretical and conceptual framework for the outcomes. The method selection and the researchers' underpinning assumption have consequences. This book will address *Diversity and Inclusion: A Framework for Research*.

The purpose

The globalization of economies, immigration, and gender awareness bring forth a need for linking GRIID to corporate social responsibility. The need for developing quality research projects that align with changing expectations with respect to equity rather than simply equality and our own background has motivated us to undertake writing this book. We will examine GRIID not as a hierarchical topology, but with a view as to construct intersectionality within the *Diversity and Inclusion: A Research Proposal Framework*. This book supports researchers of diversity and inclusion to conceptualize, identify relevant empirical evidence, interpret data, and examine topics with an intersectional perspective.

Chapter outlines

Chapter 1 provides the operational definitions, methods, and conceptual frameworks for conducting research in gender, race, identity, indigeneity, and diversity (GRIID).

Chapter 2 explains the relevance of social justice, to GRIID research, and describes the role of the researcher in creating positive social change in conducting such research.

Chapter 3 explains the research process for doctoral students and the requirements for (a) respecting human rights of participants, (b) the researcher's orientation in unfolding the meaning of data and analyzing the research findings.

Chapter 4 explores the impact of ontological and epistemological perspectives on research results on gender, race, identity, indigeneity, and diversity.

Chapter 5 examines qualitative, quantitative, and mixed methods when conducting gender, race, identity, indigeneity, and diversity, and provides some examples.

Chapter 6 explains and provides examples for writing a dissertation when conducting gender, race, identity, indigeneity, and diversity research, and describes pitfalls.

1

FRAMING THE CONVERSATION

As we embark on Chapter 1, we should note a few challenges that may muddy our discussion of gender, race, identity, indigeneity, and diversity (GRIID) research. First, we will explain identity as others have revealed to us what it means to them and the context of our findings and their implications for the identity connection to gender, race, indigeneity, and diversity. Second, as we attempt to address marginalized voices in researching topics such as indigeneity, we must draw on the already established Western and dominant views. Once we explain the basic theories and ideas, and their evolution, we will be able to suggest and develop a framework for conducting studies that can address GRIID from marginalized perspectives. We will explain the role of researcher for appropriate research in regard to social justice in Chapter 3 and how to follow ethical rules in Chapter 4, before arriving at the ontology and epistemology of a research proposal in Chapter 5, where we will discuss framing new conceptual frames. The third challenge that may create confusion is the use of word *paradigm*. Therefore, we will use *spatiotemporal epitome* as a distinct ontological and epistemological approach.

There have been numerous articles and discussions surrounding the meaning of paradigm. Although Kuhn (1996) was not the first to explain the meaning of paradigm, he was the first to construct a unique meaning: "a paradigm should be sufficiently unprecedented to a scientific way of thinking and should be open-ended in normal sciences simultaneously" (p. 10). Kuhn (1996) explained the normal sciences as disciplines such as chemistry and geology where "predominantly mathematical form can be directly compared with nature" (p. 26), not social sciences. Therefore, Kuhn argued that once there is sufficient depth and breadth with a topical area of social sciences, there is an allegorical box, a paradigm, only within which new research can proceed objectively. In defending Kuhn's definition of paradigm, an objective scientific matrix and an exemplar, Kennedy (2011) argued that "[d]iscoveries could not be explained by induction empirically but through new insights that expanded the republic of science's fund of knowledge" (p. 194).

This statement leaves the reader to wonder: If a proposition cannot be explained through empirical inductive processes, how can it be explained through insights? How do the insights manifest themselves? How would each insight's validity be examined?

Kuhn's notion of paradigm, which is used widely through social sciences, was even discredited in his own field (Percival, 1979). However, Bryant (1975) defended Kuhn's definition of paradigm as "succession of tradition-bound period punctuated by on-cumulative breaks" (p. 354). Shepherd and Challenger (2013) suggested that (a) paradigm remains a popular allegorical box among researchers in social sciences and management within which knowledge is created, (b) the paradigm incommensurability has legitimized diversity of knowledge production, and (c) paradigm discussions have led to acceptance of epistemic reflexivity where the social scientist must use a metatheoretical examination of presuppositions when arguing a point from a social location creating a habitus. Mackenzie and House (1978) argued that paradigm as explained by Kuhn is based on deductive nomological reasoning, allowing for efficiencies in conducting research in natural sciences. In general, the phenomenal world cannot be understood using paradigmatic methods (Tresch, 2001). In GRIID research where there is a vast array of approaches and weak inferences, paradigmatic approaches to research would not be possible (Mackenzie & House, 1978). Therefore, in ontological and epistemological discussions, we will refrain from using *paradigm* as a philosophical, theoretical, or conceptual frame. We will use *spatiotemporal epitome* to connote *approaches that allow for an ideal research exemplar within a particular space and time* as a distinct approach of doing things, particularly in Chapters 5 and 6.

Framing the conversation

Each scholarly conversation should make sense of what it intends to do, what is the significance of its contribution, and why it is important to have the conversation (Huff, 2009). Therefore, we should explain where we are going and identify and clarify the terms that would help us construct clear meaning, contextualizing our conversation (Creswell, 2014; Denzin & Lincoln, 2018). Definitions allow the reader to understand what the researcher means throughout the writing and provides clarity about the context in which the words are used. Thus, following our advice, first we will explain the context and then we provide definitions relevant to the context that we are providing. The approach therefore requires us to explain culture which has relevance and can contextualize what we mean by identity, gender, race, indigeneity and autochthony, diversity, and inclusion.

Identity

Identity is the center in any GRIID studies (Alvesson, Ashcraft, & Thomas, 2008); it carries a psychological, social, political, and economic connotation within a temporal framework. It is important that the researcher explains how the research would define identity and for what purpose. There are multiple ways of defining identity, depending on the purpose as used in a particular research framework. Identity may be self-defined, as a role vis-à-vis other people, or as a part of collectives such as groups or organizations (i.e., economic entities such as organizations or social, political, and cultural entities such as a community or society, encompassing various forms like tribe or a nation; Schwartz, Luyckx, & Vignoles, 2012). Some have explained individual identity in terms of principal–agent relationship where individual identity may mirror the economic interest of an organization, or the two might be closely linked (Akerlof & Kranton, 2005; Scott & Lane, 2000). In an organizational context, identity may reflect the image of organizational distinctiveness and the organizational perception by outsiders (Dutton, Dukerich, & Harquail, 1994). Organization can be applied to a work organization or, in larger context, to a society. Social identity theory (SIT) views identity as oneness with groups and organizations with the distinct affinity with the groups' or organizational attributes (Ashforth & Mael, 1989) or as a way of defining one's workspace (Ashforth & Humphrey, 1993). SIT is centered on intergroup dependencies and individual motivations, intertwining individual motivations and intergroup dependencies, defining individual identity in a singular term and group dependency simultaneously (Haslam, 2004; Tajfel, 1978; Tajfel & Turner, 1986). The SIT influences the research conversations when identity is investigated in a group, organization, or any cultural context, and we will come back to it in Chapter 4. Expanding on SIT, Cote (1996) noted that identity is linked to culture because it requires connection with the social structure, interactions with socializing institutions manifesting a pattern of behavior, and manifestation of personality that includes self, psyche, and ego.

Psychologically, identity includes a structure in different social contexts requiring researchers to clarify the term and explain the implications (van Hoof & Raaij-makers, 2003). Levine (2003) explained that "identity formation can be conceptualized as an ongoing psychosocial process during which various characteristics of the self are internalized, labeled, valued, and organized" (p. 191). Identity can also be used as a defense mechanism providing ego defenses, explaining its rationalization, denial, ideation, or symbolism (Brown & Starkey, 2000). There are, of course, other ways to describe identity.

Among several ways of defining identity is genetic, known as *identity by descent* (Browning & Browning, 2013). Lo et al. (2011) defined identity in terms of individual weakness and strength in relation to cultural attributes. Berzonsky (2016) investigated the possibility of self-definition of identity as what individuals perceive to be the meaning of life and their commitment to their purpose in life. Some political theorists have advanced the idea of political heritage as how individuals may define themselves (Morris, Mok, & Mor, 2011). Vignoles et al. (2008) conducted research based on desired and feared factors, demonstrating a temporal aspect of identity and showing that identity may be subject to change over a period. Sociologically, Kogut and Zander (1996) argued that identity can be subject to the required behavior in social division of labor. Two other areas of identity description require noting: gender and how others perceive an individual's identity. First, we will address how gender may influence identity.

Gender identity and its biological attributes was a point of contention in the 1970s at Stanford University Medical Center, where it was viewed as a disorder based on reliance on Dr. Harry Benjamin's studies from the 1960s (Fisk, 1974). A clinical study concluded that gender identity remains stable over time (Blanchard, 1988). Kroger (1997), undertaking a systematic review of psychological studies between 1966–1995, concluded that there are few gender differences in identity structure but found that identity status rather than gender in a relationship was the basis for identity formation. Condry (1984) argued that identity is dependent on gender from conception to adolescence and is influenced by biological, environmental, and social factors. Therefore, gender provides an inward examination of self-identity vis-à-vis the person's biological, social, political, and cultural orientation. It is equally important to be cognizant of how others perceive an individual, providing an outward view of individual identity.

In the 1940s, Asch (1940, 1946, 1948) discussed and conducted experiments to determine how others perceive individual identities and how identities are created externally. Several experiments by Asch (1946, 1946, 1948) determined that individuals create an identity for others by (a) evaluating characteristics that they perceive in the person they meet instantaneously, (b) comparing the individual's attributes to their own group perception of what is good or bad, and (c) assessing the individual's identity through their own experiences. Therefore, an individual's identity can externally be created based not on gender or necessarily a broad set of cultural factors but a set of individual determinations, reflecting experiences, group belonging, and a set of preset deterministic characteristics that are selected by other individuals encountering the primary subject.

Although some authors address the construction of identity as individual endeavors, others attempt to explain identity in terms of organizations and their cultures. Fadjukoff and Kroger (2016), reviewing multiple adolescence identity definitions, argued that cultural variation remains too complex in arriving at a unified description of identity based on culture. Their longitudinal study demonstrated that some aspects of identity were unstable over prolonged periods, showing diffusion with respect to politics and religion (Fadjukoff, Pulkkinen, & Kokko, 2005). SIT explains that individuals adhere to their unique identity so long as it can project a positive impression, but should that fail, individuals switch to a social identity to project a favorable view of themselves (Tajfel & Turner, 1986; Tajfel, 1978). SIT is, of course, subject to the level of conformity to a culture based on the social forces applying pressure to project certain public demeanors and behaviors irrespective of how individuals may think based on their intrinsic motivations and thinking (Bond & Smith, 1996).

Life-span theory of identity argues that individual identity is subject to sameness and continuity, and once interrupted, such as immigrants dislocated by various means, their individual identities become inflicted (Dunkel, 2005; Ertorer, 2014). Others, such as Alvesson, Ashcraft, and Thomas (2008), have viewed identity as an established reciprocal process between the individual and organization. Van Tonder and Lessing (2003) suggested that individual identity is a triangulation of individual self-definition and a relationship between self and the others and its interaction with organization. However, two challenges should be noted when individual identity is described in relation to organization. First, Gioia, Schultz, and Corley (2000) argued that organizational identity is subject to reinterpretation through time as organizational culture changes. Second, Hatch and Schultz (1997) argued that organizational identity is formulated to project a set of images. Therefore, perhaps, the best a researcher can hope for is to define the term identity as relevant to research rather than attempt to generalize identity for individual or organizational discussions in concrete cultural contexts.

Gender

Gender, legally, is based on society's normative values that present a concise definition reflecting how individuals' sex is determined, how sexes should interact, what types of acceptable biases are imposed based on sex differentiation, and how society sanctions sexual behavior (Ala Hamoudi, 2015). International bodies such as the United Nations and its agencies, before specification by the International Criminal Court (ICC) law treaty in 1998, had defined gender in biological terms (i.e., male and female) as a social construct (Oosterveld, 2005). However, the ICC after much negotiation confined its definition to male vs. female roles as defined by the cultures of respective societies negotiating the treaty (Oosterveld, 2005). Therefore, the legal concept requires a researcher conducting an international study to ground his/her argument carefully, positioning the notion of gender within the local context to clearly explain the meaning of the term for the reader.

Mwale (2008) argued that neither biological convention nor legal definition can force us into accepting such definitions as objective scientific truth. Mwale (2008) also pointed out that the social construction of biological interpretation as argued by biologists and legal experts leads to a binary heteronormative assumption of gender, forcing a set of conventions about the role of sexes in a society and disallowing other perspectives on gender. Newman (2002), in agreement with Mwale, explained that binary of definition of gender would inevitably lead to the claim of pathological behavior if one does not conform to it. Newman (2002) asserted that such a point of view would lead to dysphoria and inappropriate clinical intervention to correct gender behavior which may be very normal. Newman continued to state that although sex is a biological definition, gender is not. Gagne, Tewksbury, and McGaughey (1997) explained that gender represents an interactional system of representation to allow others socially to recognize and decode its attributes and characteristics. Building on Gagne et al.'s (1997) argument, Iorga (2015) noted that family socialization through interaction and communication creates, personifies, and strengthens the gender identity of individuals.

Defining gender can become more complicated by a myriad of issues present in various arguments. For example, some writing such as that of Al Oraimi (2011) used gender to describe the role of sexes in society, leading the reader to think that sex and gender are the same. McNay (2005) explained that various ideological perspectives muddy the gender definition based on the underlying assumptions. Claire and Alderson (2013) added that while essentialist biological theorists view gender as binary, they fail to address the question of masculinity and femininity within gender classifications. To clarify the confusion, the body and physical attributes (the ontology) is the sex while the gender is the view and psychological character (the epistemology) of how the body socially interacts (Hall, 2014; Muehlenhard & Peterson, 2011; Othman, 2015).

Race and ethnicity

Race and ethnicity is a multipronged debatable discourse. Some place its roots in economics and politics based on time and location, while others examine the issue either separately or as an inexplicable interwoven psycho-sociological temporality rooted in cultural symbols. Kant's discussion of race as part of natural history gave rise to many debates about its scientific nature, linguistic, epistemic, and ontological definition (Bernasconi, 2010). Regardless of the perspective, the debate among scholars have been raging about its scientific foundation (Banton, 1999; 2010; Bernasconi, 2010). Some see race and ethnicity as two distinct axes of power-structure in a sociological context (Valdez & Golash-Boza, 2017; Valluvan & Kapoor, 2016). Therefore, theoretically and based on application, divergence of views about race, ethnicity, and their connectedness continues.

Scholars have continued to view race and its definition from various perspectives. Banton (2010) viewed race as human classification and taxonomic. Hiernaux (1965) did not agree with Banton, arguing that race is not a classification but a concept that can be perceived differently by everyone. Lentin (2016), expanding Hiernaux's argument, noted that some formations of the race concept can be historical while others can be ahistorical, and some of its attributes can be "frozen" while others can be "motile." Golash-Boza (2013), building on Feagin and Elias's (2013) discussions, argued that race can only be explained in light of systemic racism exposing its nature and existence. Philosophically, race has been seen as a way of making injustices invisible and providing cover for acts of colonialism and slavery (Zeynep, 2017). Wimmer (2015) asserted that rather than accepting any of these ideas as axiomatic truth, we must dissect their assumptions. Yet the concept of race remains as elusive as ever (Winant, 2006), even in law (Young, 2009).

Aranda (2017) argued that while ethnicity implies inclusion or assimilation, race signifies exclusion which impacts the arguments about identity, group relationships with members, and social justice regarding access and resources. Aranda (2017) pointed out that although race and ethnicity imply different context when used together, ethnoracial perspective allows comparison of one group vis-à-vis another—for example, Black vs. Spanish—and investigation of privileges and hierarchies within a group.

Baehler (2002) argued that when formulating social policies, ethnicity as an identifying mark disappears as one introduces demographic information such as income level, age, marital status, and literacy. Baehler (2002) further asserted that factors such as lower education has a higher relationship to variables such as employment and, hence, ethnicity as a factor becomes indistinguishable. Baehler cautions that when comparing Māori in New Zealand and Blacks in the United States, lower education can be a direct effect of lack of access by ethnic groups.

Indigeneity and autochthony

Indigeneity and autochthony can be described in different ways depending on the discipline, the domain of inquiry, and the topic at hand. The genetic argument fought in the name of science by Wells against the Australian aboriginal, Singh's righteousness of knowing where his people came from provides the backdrop to the landscape of the controversy surrounding the question of indigeneity (Reardon & TallBear, 2012). The kaleidoscope of definitions covers a range of disciplines from social sciences to genetics and medicine.

Anthropology has been one of domains involved in defining indigeneity. De Jongh (2006) addressed the complexities of South African ethnicities, explaining that indigeneity owes its roots to sociopolitical dynamics within different periods based on the juxtaposition of perceptions and unpacking the meaning of ethnicity. De Jongh (2006) argued that indigeneity can only be addressed within a case study providing specificity based on location and sociopolitical context. Sociopolitical discussions have prompted scholars to examine the concept of autochthony and allochthony. Yanow and van der Haar (2009) used autochthony and allochthony as binary terms to distinguish between native and foreign born while addressing Dutch government policies. Yanow and van der Haar (2009) equated allochthon to a U.S. hyphenated national distinction such as Irish-American.

Inclusion and diversity

While diversity addresses the differences based on individual attributes and or social relationships (Nishii 2013; Roberson, 2006), inclusion is a systemic effort to include differences in collectives such as groups, organizations, tribes, and societies for a particular objective (e.g., meeting government requirements, improving work engagement, improving social relationships in a society). Inclusion requires accepting the differences without individuals sacrificing or hiding any of their individual attributes or characteristics as a condition of acceptance (Mor Barak, 2015).

Inclusion

Inclusion requires perception of acceptance by individuals and groups with their unique attributes and array of differences and allowing them equal access to the processes and resources (Mor Barak, 2015). One study defined inclusion at organizational level as seeking out, respecting, and valuing unique individual knowledge and experiences, allowing individuals to feel included and contribute to their full potential (Roberson, 2006). Ferdman (2017) defined inclusion as "a process and practice that involves working with diversity as a resource" (p. 235). Vanderstraeten (2013) argued that inclusion at a societal level requires establishment of governmental policies and processes in addition to social norms allowing for full participation by each individual. Clarifying the concept of inclusion as defined by Vanderstraeten (2013), Faist (2009) noted that inclusion does not mean to incorporate but rather deconstructing the notion of dominance and allowing for pluralism and multiculturalism. Humpage (2006) extended the inclusion argument to colonized societies by White settlers, arguing that White settlers through establishment of social norms, policies, and processes in New Zealand did not allow for inclusion of individuals from the Māori tribes. Denial of inclusion has been equally applied to other colonized groups such as Native Americans (Ladson-Billings & Donnor, 2005), African Americans (Madison, 2005), Australian aboriginals (Kemmis & McTaggart, 2005), etc. The various approaches to inclusion can also present unique challenges.

There are several challenges in using inclusion. For example, as Doyle and George (2008) argued, inclusion is about access to the historically under-represented, which may shift the focus from equity to equality, from distributive to procedural justice, skewing the essence of inclusion. Others such as Azoulay (1997) viewed inclusion as an incorrect term in a society where ideas such as Nazi ideology required inclusion in the mix representing freedom of speech. Terms such as *multivocality* to denote representation of ideas and cultures while respecting social justice and legitimate ideologies have been suggested (Azoulay, 1997). As Palacios (2016) pointed out, there is currently a lack of procedural clarity in inclusion practices, creating obstacles in democratizing access for success based on distributive and procedural justice, as observed globally.

Diversity

Talcott Parson in response to Weber and Durkheim (as cited in Vanderstraeten, 2013) argued that the need for addressing diversity was originally due to the secularization of religions, using the word etymologically. Talcott Parson argued that diversity, sociologically as a set of extrinsic values, requires recognition of different value systems and dynamics respecting different ideas while maintaining a broad understanding of how distinct groups with different ideologies can function together (Vanderstraeten, 2013). However, diversity can take many forms, following different paths such as cultural, functional, and neurodiversity.

Cultural diversity in its simplest form represents the differences in appearance of clothing articles, cuisine, arts, and mannerisms (Moodley, 1983). At the most basic level, there are two types of diversity. Intrinsically, diversity is the manifestation of differences based on individuals' cognition, perception of reality, and emotional, psychological, and biological state. Extrinsically, diversity is the differences in the way individuals categorize themselves as a part of groups, gender identities, ethnicities, races, tribes, nationalities, societies and social structures, cultures, and belief systems such as religion. However, the literature on diversity provides additional complexities, often crossing the intrinsic and extrinsic lines of defining diversity. While some have advanced the idea that psychology is the science dedicated to understanding diversity as intrinsic individual attributes and its nuances (Mendoza-Denton & España, 2010), others have argued that diversity is simultaneously anthropological, where individual characteristics are the marks for identifying diversity (Mor Barak, 2015). Yet others such as Blau (1980) theorized that diversity is simultaneous psychological and anthropological differences with various degrees and shades. Applying Blau's definition to workplace, Biemann and Kearney (2010) described diversity as the degrees of separation, variety, and disparity, and its dimensions rest in the mind of the researcher. Zhang and Goldberg (2014) noted that diversity is the individual sensitivity to elimination of uncertainty based on identity in fitting the environment in which he or she operates that can be applicable to society at large or in an organization. Burns and Ulrich (2016) simply defined workplace diversity as divergence in thinking rather than the social definition which focuses on social justice.

Jimenez (2010) viewed diversity as malleable phenomenon based on ethnic heritage that can coalesce around the dominant view in a society subject to temporality. Grillo (2007), distinguished between diversity and difference while examining the British government's policies on integration. Grillo (2007) noted that while diversity requires and stands as opposition to integration, differences will remain as such without resolution. Voyer (2011) described diversity as a platform for mediating individual identities regarding it. Roberson (2006) summed up diversity as unique differences, encompassing different ways that people may differ and variation of observable and non-observable difference. Burri (2010) defined cultural diversity "as incorporating a distinct set of policy objectives and choices at the global level" (p. 1060). Internationally, Faist (2009) observed diversity as the result of "disaggregation of territories, political control, and cultural practices" (p. 172). Zhao and Cao (2010) explained diversity as the deviance based on anomie theory, regardless of the differences of approach by Durkheim and Merton. Van Ewijk (2011) saw diversity as contextual, applicable to specific empirical research without any explicit definition encompassing all situations. Ferdman (1995) noted that diversity can be rooted in individual or group differences based on psychological, social, and cultural differences.

Culture

Researchers use culture in contextualizing GRIID research. However, culture includes a broad range of definitions based on disciplinary focus and the context. Drearley (1941), without directly defining the attributes of culture, argued that social forces influence it primarily in two unusual ways. First, Drearley (1941) pointed out that the speed of social dynamics has an inverse relationship with the groups' conflict within the same culture. Second, Drearley added that the slower the rate of social dynamics changes, the lower the likelihood of the biological differences as a primary antagonism between groups within that culture. Kroeber and

Kluckhohn (1952) compiled over 150 definitions of cultures used invariably by different disciplines. Blau (1980), in an imaginative tale of the discovery of a new star, theorized that perhaps our lack of understanding of a culture is due to either our lack of connectedness to it or a lack of grasping the differences within it by its groups. Leung (1989) argued that in examining cultural differences, (a) one should explore the relationship between cultural differences and cultural processes and (b) culture must be unpacked or deglobalized. Baldwin et al. (2005) defined culture based on three cultivation themes: (a) as general individuals' intellectual, spiritual, and aesthetic development; (b) a particular way of life by a group of people, or based on a particular period; and (c) as it relates to art forms, music, literature, sculpture, and theatre. Therefore, as an integral part of defining any component of the GRIID, researchers should be mindful of its cultural context.

A recent rendition of culture's definition has been created by Geert Hofstede in collaboration with others. Hofstede, Hofstede, and Minkov (2010), taking the positivist and Eurocentric view, explained cultures as "the differences in thinking, feeling, and acting of people around the globe" (p. 4). They call "such patterns of thinking, feeling, and acting mental programs" or *software of the mind* that represent the collective programming (Hofstede et al., 2010, pp. 5–6). The authors viewed the practice of culture as the use of symbolism, heroes, rituals, and values capable of reproducing itself. Hofstede et al. (2010) categorized culture into national, regional or ethnic, religious or linguistic, gender, generation, social class—and for those employed, organizational, departmental, or corporate levels (p. 18)—claiming that time would not impact its core structure despite the superficial changes (p. 19) and can only be defined by national boundaries not tribalism or any other means (p. 21). Hofstede et al. (2010) asserted that comparative cultural studies belong to normal science as explained by Kuhn (1996).

Baldwin et al. (2005) argued that irrespective of the way one goes about defining culture, one cannot point to it as a set of concrete attributes collectively shared, demonstrating a particular set of behavior as a positivist would wish it to be, demonstrating individuals' conscious or unconscious behavior all the time. In 2014, an examination of the concept of culture, while re-emphasizing its vagueness even as stated in the United Nation's reports, suggested that culture is a dichotomous story of binary human development where the Western view and the rest attempt to fight for hegemonic epistemological and political position (Telleria, 2015). Therefore, we like to remind researchers that they must provide clear parameters and establish specific criteria for defining culture to correctly and clearly contextualize the GRIID within the discipline and the domain of inquiry or explain its relevance.

Connecting the dots: from identity to culture

Various dissertation undertakings, regardless of discipline or focus, require a set of assumptions about one or multiple components of GRIID. Examination of identities requires contextual understanding of their association with place, time, and the roles individuals are positioned in (Hagan, 2006; Hall, 2017). For example, Informant 4 and 6 stated that *color as ethnicity had to be separated from race* to explain their identities in terms of changes in location. Therefore, as a researcher undertakes the investigation of any of the GRIID topics, relationships between its various components should be clearly delineated and explained for the researched so they understand the nature of questions asked, and for the reader who is attempting to make sense of the data and its analysis within its proper context.

Summary

Before examining gender, race, identity, indigeneity, and diversity (GRIID), the researcher should define the particular context used, their temporality, and how the research would advance the knowledge base in a domain of inquiry. Due to the enormity of the GRIID field, the researcher must narrow the investigation as much as possible and confine the work to one discipline. Also, the researcher should explain why the approach was selected, and how the findings would help expand the existing literature on the topic. Once the researcher defines the terms, provides the context, and narrows the topic to one discipline and some sort of topic within that discipline, she should identify a spatiotemporal epitome for addressing the topic.

EXERCISES

Review the GRIID literature

a   Narrow the focus to a discipline within which you intend to expand the literature if you are part of PhD program (if you are in a practice-based degree program, use a work problem as a starting point).

b   Review the literature for gaps that can help identify a problem and help expand the existing literature.

c   As you review the literature, review the references within each article or book and use a cascading principle to expand your search for a comprehensive review of each term.

d   Define the required terms necessary for the research undertaking, and review their historical evolution, opposing views on each definition, and lens (e.g., postcolonialism, decolonizing, and poststructuralist) used in examining them.

e   Explain the terms' relevance to the topic within the GRIID study you intend to carry out.

References

Akerlof, G. A., & Kranton, R. E. (2005). Identity and the Economics of Organizations. *Journal of Economic Perspectives*, 19(1), 9–32.

Ala Hamoudi, H. (2015). Sex and the shari'a: Defining gender norms and sexual deviancy in Shi'i Islam. *Fordham International Law Journal*, 39(25).

Al Oraimi, S. Z. (2011). The Concept of Gender in Emirati Culture: An Analytical Study of the Role of the State in Redefining Gender and Social Roles. *Museum International*, 63(3/4), 78–92. doi:10.1111/muse.12009

Alvesson, M., Ashcraft, K. L., & Thomas, R. (2008). Identity matters: Reflections on the construction of identity scholarship in organization studies. *Organization*, 15(1), 5–28.

Aranda, E. (2017). An ethnoracial perspective: Response to Valdez and Golash-Boza. *Ethnic & Racial Studies*, 40(13), 2232–2239. doi:10.1080/01419870.2017.1344264

Asch, S. E. (1940). Studies in the Principles of Judgements and Attitudes: II. Determination of Judgements by Group and by Ego Standards. *Journal of Social Psychology*, 12(2), 433.

Asch, S. (1946). Forming Impressions of Personality. *Journal of Abnormal and Social Psychology*, 41(3), 258–290.

Asch, S. E. (1948). The doctrine of suggestion, prestige and imitation in social psychology. *Psychological Review*, 55(5), 250–276. doi:10.1037/h0057270

Ashforth, B. E., & Humphrey, R. H. (1993). Emotional labor in service roles: The influence of identity. *Academy of Management Review*, 18(1), 88–115.

Ashforth, B. E., & Mael, F. (1989). Social Identity Theory and the Organization. *Academy of Management Review*, 14(1), 20–39. doi:10.5465/AMR.1989.4278999

Azoulay, K. G. (1997). Experience, Empathy and Strategic Essentialism. *Cultural Studies*, 11(1), 89–110.

Baehler, K. (2002). Ethnicity-based research and politics: Snapshots from the United States and New Zealand. *Social Policy Journal of New Zealand*, 18.

Baldwin, J. R., Faulkner, S. L., Hecht, M. L., & Lindsley, S. L. (Eds.). (2005). *Redefining Culture: Perspectives Across the Disciplines*. Mahwah, NJ: Lawrence Erlbaum Associates.

Banton, M. (1999). Racism today: A perspective from international politics. *Ethnic & Racial Studies*, 22(3), 606.

Banton, M. (2010). The Vertical and Horizontal Dimensions of the Word Race. *Ethnicities*, 10(1), 127–140.

Bernasconi, R. (2010). Defining Race Scientifically. *Ethnicities*, 10(1), 141–148.

Berzonsky, M. D. (2016). An Exploration of Personal Assumptions About Self-Construction and Self-Discovery. *Identity*, 16(4), 267. doi:10.1080/15283488.2016.1229609

Biemann, T., & Kearney, E. (2010). Size Does Matter: How Varying Group Sizes in a Sample Affect the Most Common Measures of Group Diversity. *Organizational Research Methods*, 13(3), 582–599.

Blanchard, R. (1988). Nonhomosexual Gender Dysphoria. *The Journal of Sex Research*, 24(1–4), 188–193.

Blau, P. M. (1980). A Fable about Social Structure. *Social Forces*, 58(3), 777–788.

Bond, R., & Smith, P. B. (1996). Culture and conformity: A meta-analysis of studies using Asch's (1952b, 1956) line judgment task. *Psychological Bulletin*, 119(1), 111–137.

Brown, A. D., & Starkey, K. (2000). Organizational identity and learning: A psychodynamic perspective. *The Academy of Management Review*, 25(1), 102–120. doi:10.2307/259265

Browning, B. L., & Browning, S. R. (2013). Improving the Accuracy and Efficiency of Identity-by-Descent Detection in Population Data. *Genetics*, 194(2), 459–471.

Bryant, C. A. (1975). Kuhn, paradigms and sociology. *British Journal of Sociology*, September, 354–359.

Burns, W. E., & Ulrich, D. (2016). The evolving diversity agenda. *Strategic HR Review*, 15(5), 220. doi:10.1108/SHR-08-2016-0065

Burri, M. (2010). Cultural Diversity as a Concept of Global Law: Origins, Evolution and Prospects. *Diversity*, 2(8), 1059–1084. doi:10.3390/d2081059

Claire, C. C., & Alderson, K. G. (2013). Living Outside the Gender Binary: A Phenomenological Exploration into the Lived Experience of Female Masculinity. *Canadian Journal of Counselling & Psychotherapy*, 47(1), 49–70.

Condry, J. C. (1984). Gender Identity and Social Competence. *Sex Roles*, 11(5–6), 485.

Cote, J. E. (1996). Sociological perspectives on identity formation: the culture-identity link and identity capital. *Journal of Adolescence*, 19(5), 417–428.

Creswell, John W. (2014). *Research Design: Qualitative, Quantitative, and Mixed Methods Approaches*. Thousand Oaks, CA: SAGE Publications.

de Jongh, M. (2006). Exclusivity, hybridity and community: Negotiating place, ethnicity and South African realities. *Anthropology Southern Africa*, 29(3–4), 74–83.

Denzin, N. K., & Lincoln, Y. S. (2018). *The Sage Handbook of Qualitative Research* (5th ed.). Los Angeles, CA: SAGE Publications.

Drearley, H. C. (1941). Culture Change and Race Relations. *Social Forces*, 20(2), 260–263.

Doyle, R., & George, U. (2008). Achieving and Measuring Diversity: An Organizational Change Approach. *Social Work Education*, 27(1), 97–110. doi:10.1080/02615470601141235

Dunkel, C. S. (2005). The Relation Between Self-Continuity and Measures of Identity. *Identity*, 5(1), 21. doi:10.1207/s1532706xid0501_2

Dutton, J. E., Dukerich, J. M., & Harquail, C. V. (1994). Organizational Images and Member Identification. *Administrative Science Quarterly*, 39(2), 239–263.

Ertorer, S. E. (2014). Managing Identity in the Face of Resettlement. *Identity*, 14(4), 268. doi:10.1080/15283488.2014.944695

Fadjukoff, P., & Kroger, J. (2016). Identity Development in Adulthood: Introduction. *Identity*, 16(1), 1–7. doi:10.1080/15283488.2015.1121821

Fadjukoff, P., Pulkkinen, L., & Kokko, K. (2005). Identity Processes in Adulthood: Diverging Domains. *Identity*, 5(1), 1. doi:10.1207/s1532706xid0501_1

Faist, T. (2009). Diversity—a new mode of incorporation? *Ethnic & Racial Studies*, 32(1), 171–190. doi:10.1080/01419870802483650

Feagin, J., & Elias, S. (2013). Rethinking racial formation theory: a systemic racism critique. *Ethnic & Racial Studies*, 36(6), 931–960. doi:10.1080/01419870.2012.669839

Ferdman, B. M. (1995). Cultural Identity and Diversity in Organizations. In M. Chemers, S. Oskamp, & M. Constanzo (Eds.). (1995). *Diversity in Organizations: New Perspectives for a Changing Workplace* (Vol. 8). Thousand Oaks, CA: SAGE Publications.

Ferdman, B. M. (2017). Paradoxes of inclusion: understanding and managing the tensions of diversity and multiculturalism. *Journal of Applied Behavioral Science*, 53(2), 235.

Fisk, N. M. (1974). Editorial: Gender dysphoria syndrome—the conceptualization that liberalizes indications for total gender reorientation and implies a broadly based multidimensional rehabilitative regimen. *The Western Journal of Medicine*, 120(5), 386–391.

Gagne, P., Tewksbury, R., & McGaughey, D. (1997). Coming out and crossing over: Identity formation and proclamation in a transgender community. *Gender & Society*, 11(4), 478–508.

Gioia, D. A., Schultz, M., & Corley, K. G. (2000). Organizational Identity, Image, and Adaptive Instability. *Academy of Management Review*, 25(1), 63–81. doi:10.5465/AMR.2000.2791603

Golash-Boza, T. (2013). Does racial formation theory lack the conceptual tools to understand racism? *Ethnic & Racial Studies*, 36(6), 994–999. doi:10.1080/01419870.2013.767919

Grillo, R. (2007). An excess of alterity? Debating difference in a multicultural society. *Ethnic and Racial Studies*, 30(6), 979–998.

Hagan, J. (2006). Negotiating Social Membership in the Contemporary World. *Social Forces*, 85(2), 631–642.

Hall, J. (2014). Unpacking 'Gender Issues' Research. *Philosophy of Mathematics Education Journal*, 28, 1–10.

Hall, S. M. (2017). Mooring 'super-diversity' to a brutal migration milieu. *Ethnic & Racial Studies*, 40(9), 1562–1573. doi:10.1080/01419870.2017.1300296

Haslam, S. A. (2004). *Psychology in Organizations: The Social Identity Approach*. London: SAGE Publications.

Hatch, M. J., & Schultz, M. (1997). Relations between organizational culture, identity and image. *European Journal of Marketing*, 31(5–6), 356–365. doi:10.1108/eb060636

Hiernaux, J. (1965). Problems of race definition. *International Social Science Journal*, 17(1), 115–117.

Hofstede, G., Hofstede, G. J., & Minkov, M. (2010). *Cultures and Organizations: Software of the Mind* (3rd. ed.). New York: McGraw-Hill.

Huff, A. S. (2009). *Designing Research for Publication*. Los Angeles, CA: SAGE Publications.

Humpage, L. (2006). An 'inclusive' society: A 'leap forward' for Māori in New Zealand? *Critical Social Policy*, 26(1), 220–242. doi:10.1177/0261018306059773

Iorga, A. M. (2015). The Role of Family Socializing in Building Gender Identity. *Scientific Papers Series: Management, Economic Engineering In Agriculture And Rural Development*, 15(2), 161–166.

Jimenez, T. R. (2010). Affiliative ethnic identity: A more elastic link between ethnic ancestry and culture. *Ethnic & Racial Studies*, 33(10), 1756–1775. doi:10.1080/01419870100367855l

Kemmis, S., & McTaggart, R. (2005). Participatory Action Research: Communicative Action and Public Policy. In N. K. Denzin & Y. S. Lincoln (Eds.), *The Sage Handbook of Qualitative Research* (3rd ed., pp. 559–604). Thousand Oaks, CA: SAGE Publications.

Kennedy, T. (2011). From Paradigms to 'Paideia': Thomas S. Kuhn and Michael Polanyi in Conversation. *Bulletin of Science, Technology & Society*, 31(3), 193–199.

Kogut, B. K., & Zander, U. I. (1996). What Firms Do? Coordination, Identity, and Learning. *Organization Science*, 7(5), 502–518.

Kroeber, A. L., & Kluckhohn, C. (1952). *Culture: A Critical Review of Concepts and Definitions*. Cambridge, MA: Peabody Museum.

Kroger, J. (1997). Gender and identity: the intersection of structure, content, and context. *Sex Roles*, 36, 747–770.

Kuhn, T. S. (1996). *The Structure of Scientific Revolution* (3rd ed.). Chicago: University of Chicago Press.

Ladson-Billings, G., & Donnor, J. (2005). The Moral Activist Role of Critical Race Theory Scholarship. In N. K. Denzin & Y. S. Lincoln (Eds.), *The Sage Handbook of Qualitative Research* (3rd ed., pp. 279–302). Thousand Oaks, CA: SAGE Publications.

Lentin, A. (2016). Racism in public or public racism: Doing anti-racism in 'post-racial' times. *Ethnic and Racial Studies*, 39(1), 33–48. doi:10.1080/01419870.2016.1096409

Leung, K. (1989). Cross-cultural differences: Individual-level vs. culture-level analysis. *International Journal of Psychology*, 24(6), 703–719. doi:10.1080/00207598908247840

Levine, C. (2003). Introduction: Structure, Development, and Identity Formation. *Identity*, 3(3), 191.

Lo, C., Helwig, C. C., Chen, S. X., Ohashi, M. M., & Cheng, C. M. (2011). A Needs-Based Perspective on Cultural Differences in Identity Formation. *Identity*, 11(3), 211. doi:10.1080/15283488.2011.594782

Mackenzie, K. D., & House, R. (1978). Paradigm Development in the Social Sciences: A Proposed Research Strategy. *Academy of Management Review*, 3(1), 7.

McNay, L. (2005). Agency and experience: Gender as a lived relation. *Sociological Review Monograph*, 53(1), 174–190.

Madison, D. S. (2005). Critical Ethnography as Street Performance: Reflection of Home, Race, Murder, and Justice. In N. K. Denzin & Y. S. Lincoln (Eds.), *The Sage Handbook of Qualitative Research* (3rd ed., pp. 537–546). Thousand Oaks, CA: SAGE Publications.

Mendoza-Denton, R., & España, C. (2010). Diversity science: What is it? *Psychological Inquiry*, 21(2), 140–145. doi:10.1080/10478401003800945

Moodley, K. (1983). Canadian multiculturalism as ideology. *Ethnic & Racial Studies*, 6(3), 320.

Mor Barak, M. E. (2015). Inclusion is the Key to Diversity Management, but What is Inclusion? *Human Service Organizations: Management, Leadership & Governance*, 39(2), 83–88. doi:10.1080/23303131.2015.1035599

Morris, M. W., Mok, A., & Mor, S. (2011). Cultural Identity Treat: The Role of Cultural Identifications in Moderating Closure Responses to Foreign Cultural Inflow. *Journal of Social Issues*, 67(4), 760–773. doi:10.1111/j.1540-4560.2011.01726.x

Muehlenhard, C., & Peterson, Z. (2011). Distinguishing Between Sex and Gender: History, Current Conceptualizations, and Implications. *Sex Roles*, 64(11–12), 791–803. doi:10.1007/s11199-011-9932-5

Mwale, S. (2008). What Contributions Have Biological Approaches Made to Our Understanding of Gender and Sexuality? *Journal of Social & Psychological Sciences*, 1(2), 88–96.

Newman, L. K. (2002). Sex, gender and culture: Issues in the definition, assessment and treatment of gender identity disorder. *Clinical Child Psychology and Psychiatry*, 7(3), 352–359. doi:10.1177/1359104502007003004

Nishii, L. H. (2013). The benefits of climate for inclusion for gender-diverse groups. *Academy of Management Journal*, 56, 1754–1774. doi:10.5465/amj.2009.0823

Omi, M. & Winant, H. (1994). *Racial Formations*. New York: Routledge.

Othman, J. A. (2015). Constituting gender, locating the body. *Journal of Gender Studies*, 24(6), 634–643. doi:10.1080/09589236.2013.866036

Oosterveld, V. (2005). The Definition of 'Gender' in the Rome Statute of the International Criminal Court: A Step Forward or Back for International Criminal Justice? *Harvard Human Rights Journal*, 18, 55–84.

Palacios, J. M. (2016). Equality and diversity in democracy: how can we democratizeinclusively? *Equality, Diversity and Inclusion: An International Journal*, 35(5–6), 350–363, doi:10.1108/EDI-04-2016-0030

Percival, W. K. (1979). The Applicability of Kuhn's Paradigms to the Social Sciences. *American Sociologist*, 14(1), 28–31.

Reardon, J., & TallBear, K. (2012). Your DNA Is Our History. *Current Anthropology*, 53(S5), S233. doi:10.1086/662629

Roberson, Q. M. (2006). Disentangling the meanings of diversity and inclusion in organizations. *Group & Organization Management*, 31(2), 212–236.

Schwartz, S. J., Luyckx, K., & Vignoles, V. L. (2012). *Handbook of Identity Theory and Research: Domains and Categories*. New York: Springer Science+Business Media.

Scott, S. G., & Lane, V. R. (2000). A Stakeholder Approach to Organizational Identity. *Academy of Management Review*, 25(1), 45–62.

Shepherd, C., & Challenger, R. (2013). Revisiting Paradigm(s) in Management Research: A Rhetorical Analysis of the Paradigm Wars. *International Journal of Management Reviews*, 15(2), 225–244. doi:10.1111/ijmr.12004

Tajfel, H. (1978). Social categorization, social identity, and social comparisons. In H. Tajfel (Ed.), *Differentiation between Groups* (pp. 61–76). London: Academic Press.

Tajfel, H., & Turner, J. (1986). The social identity theory of intergroup relations. In S. Worchel & W. Austin (Eds.), *Psychology of Intergroup Relations* (2nd ed., pp. 7–17). Chicago: Nelson-Hall.

Telleria, J. (2015). What Does Culture Mean for the UNDP? *Cultural Studies*, 29(2), 255–271. doi:10.1080/09502386.2014.900100

Tresch, J. (2001). On Going Native: Thomas Kuhn and Anthropological Method. *Philosophy of the Social Sciences*, 31(3), 302–322.

Valdez, Z., & Golash-Boza, T. (2017). Towards an intersectionality of race and ethnicity. *Ethnic & Racial Studies*, 40(13), 2256–2261. doi:10.1080/01419870.2017.1344277

Valluvan, S., & Kapoor, N. (2016). Notes on theorizing racism and other things. *Ethnic & Racial Studies*, 39(3), 375–382. doi:10.1080/01419870.2016.1109680

Vanderstraeten, R. (2013). Talcott Parsons and the enigma of secularization. *European Journal of Social Theory*, 16(1), 69–84. doi:10.1177/1368431012449236

van Ewijk, A. R. (2011). Diversity and diversity policy: Diving into fundamental differences. *Journal of Organizational Change Management*, 24(5), 680. doi:10.1108/09534811111158921

van Hoof, A., & Raaijmakers, Q. W. (2003). The Search for the Structure of Identity Formation. *Identity*, 3(3), 271–289.

Van Tonder, C.L. & Lessing, B. C. (2003). From identity to organisation identity: The evolution of a concept. *SA Journal of Industrial Psychology*, 29(2). doi:10.4102/sajip.v29i2.99

Vignoles, V. L., Manzi, C., Regalia, C., Jemmolo, S., & Scabini, E. (2008). Identity motives underlying desired and feared possible future selves. *Journal of Personality*, 76(5), 1165–1200. doi:10.1111/j.1467-6494.2008.00518.x

Voyer, A. (2011). Disciplined to diversity: learning the language of multiculturalism. *Ethnic and Racial Studies*, 34(11), 1874–1893.

Wimmer, A. (2015). Race-centrism: A critique and a research agenda. *Ethnic and Racial Studies*, 38(13), 2186–2205. doi:10.1080/01419870.2015.1058510

Winant, H. (2006). Race and racism: Towards a global future. *Ethnic and Racial Studies*, 29(5), 986–1003. doi:10.1080/01419870600814031

Yanow, D., & Van der Haar, M. (2009). People Out of Place: Allochthony and Autochthony in Netherlands Identity Discourse—Metaphors and Categories in Action. *Conference Papers—International Studies Association*, 1–43.

Young, D. E. (2009). Defining Race through Law: Enforcing the Social Norms of Power and Privilege. *Albany Law Review*, 72(4), 1041–1046.

Zeynep, D. (2017). Critical Philosophy of Race as Political Phenomenology: Questions for Robert Bernasconi. *Comparative & Continental Philosophy*, 9(2), 130. doi:10.1080/17570638.2017.1331917

Zhang, L., & Goldberg, C. (2014). Sensitivity-to-diversity: A moderator of diversity—affective outcomes relationships. *Equality, Diversity & Inclusion*, 33(6), 494–509. doi:10.1108/EDI-05-2013-0028

Zhao, R., & Cao, L. (2010). Social Change and Anomie: A Cross-National Study. *Social Forces*, 88(3), 1209–1230.

2

ROLE OF SOCIAL JUSTICE AND THE RESEARCHER

Knowledge generating in social sciences is based on the existential reality of political economy, ideology, and the exchange between the research subject and the researcher, requiring contextualization or connecting the dots (Fine & Weis, 2005; Greenwood & Levin, 2005). Contextualization must be meaningful and precise. For example, when conducting research in an indigenous setting, the researcher must recognize the appearance of things such as representation of values, genealogy, and the cultural view of the researched subject from the world without (Bishop, 2005; Smith 2005). Another example would be the way a researcher applies a conceptual frame to make sense of the data presented. For instance, feminism—which used a singular axis of power in examining issues and traditionally had an in-built bias against gays, lesbians, women of color, and colonized—now uses multiple power axes, providing a more holistic approach in examining the subjects and data (Pollack & Eldridge, 2016) and influencing the type of social justice that is produced as result of inquiry.

It is important to note that even when one conducts quantitative research in social sciences, contextualization is required (Walter & Anderson, 2013). Therefore, we will first define what we mean by social justice and positive social change (as the outcome of the research). Second, we will examine the implication of justice for the researcher's approach to conducting gender, race, identity, indigeneity, and diversity (GRIID) investigation, the study's intent, and analyzing the results. As we move through this chapter, we will present scenarios to illustrate the way social justice should be addressed and how to conduct GRIID research to provide positive social impact.

Social justice

In a broad context, the social scientist's responsibility is to address and mitigate disposition of social justice as a matter of pragmatism (Frohlich, 2007). *Social justice* may be explained based on different theories and approaches. For example, equity theory explains that in a social exchange, the proportionality of perceived outcome to input determines the social justice dispensed, and the individual who intentionally perceives the more deserved outcome to input will be the exploiter and the other individual would be the victim (Mahoney, 2013; Walster & Walster, 1975). When unpacking equity theory and applying the concept to social science research, the perception of the observer, the allocator, and the rewardee in respect to equity based on normative assumptions and individual cognitive processing of fairness must be examined to arrive at a relatively true outcome (van den Bos et al., 2015). Perhaps to address proportionality of justice when conducting research in social science, in general and more specifically in GRIID, the researcher's engagement in the process—for example, participatory action research—can help restore a sense of fairness by all parties affected (Koirala-Azad, & Fuentes, 2009; Zapata-Sepulveda, Jara-Labarthe, & Espinoza-Verdejo, 2014). Providing context for social justice requires us to define what we mean by it from a philosophical and historical perspective.

The researcher must be concerned with two aspects of justice. First, as Deutsch (2006) explained, justice is the absence of oppression in any form that may not even be violent or tyrannical. Oppression is the result of "distributive injustice, procedural injustice, retributive injustice, moral exclusion, and cultural imperialism" (Deutsch, 2006, p. 10). Second, reaction to justice may be (a) camouflaged whereas reaction to injustice may be very pronounced (Colquitt et al., 2015), and (b) the individual perception of unfair equity in dispensation of justice may lead to individual anger (Stouten, Kuppens, & Decoster, 2013). Therefore, the researcher must be cognizant and clearly explain the framework within which the research is conducted to clarify and explicate any bias that may be introduced into the study by the researcher and the researched. The information about the effects of social justice bias in GRIID studies is required as a pretext to methodology to visibly shelter the study from any undue influences. Let us examine the impact in qualitative and quantitative study scenarios.

SCENARIO (a): QUALITATIVE STUDY

Let us assume that we are conducting research examining the results of the Australian social security administration policies on the unemployment conditions of aboriginals. In such research, to adequately address social justice in creating positive social change, the problem should be framed as, for example: How can modifications in the Australian social security system improve the unemployment for the aboriginal/improve living conditions/enhance quality of life? The problem statement would allow us to frame the entire inquiry to arrive at an outcome that can serve the indigenous needs, allowing the researcher to collect data and analyze them to make positive social change for the indigenous population rather than trying to fit their needs into the wider Australian society. However, slight changes in the problem statement would change the purpose of the research and may have a negative impact. For example, stating the problem as "The specific problem is a clear understanding of effective application of the Australian social security policies to aboriginal population" uses language that implies how to force the aboriginals into the system rather than how to make the system fair for them.

SCENARIO (b): QUANTITATIVE STUDY

Let us assume we are conducting research to determine the relationship between women's social identity and the possibility of incarceration. In this type of quantitative study, setting the context for creating hypotheses, the construct of each hypothesis, the instruments used to test the relationship, and analysis of the data can produce positive social change through crafting the hypotheses to include some form of social justice implication for women and analyzing the findings to determine how social justice can benefit the women.

Social justice provides an objective view of GRIID research because it is not subject to political bargaining, nor can it be used as a *"calculus of social interest"* (Rawls, 2005, p. 4). Weitz (1993) argued that Rawls's definition of social justice is inadequate, especially as one realizes that social justice is the result of rationalization of the state of the society rather than what one faces. Therefore, social justice, as Weitz (1993) viewed it and we concur with her, is the existential projection of academic ideas rationalizing it in whatever form is manifested. In addition, Rawls's reliance on highly evolved institutions in guaranteeing procedural justice cannot address the needs of societies with a conglomeration of tribes, ethnicities, indigenous and immigrant, marginalized by sex and gender identity, and autochthonous and allochthonous citizens to receive justice (Berkey, 2016) as they attempt to liberate themselves from the colonial heritage and find a socio-economic and political footing without developed institutions. Thus, the GRIID researcher must be aware of the role he or she plays in creating and embodying social justice. Perhaps a scenario can help us better explain the case in point.

SCENARIO: THE RESEARCH

Imagine that a researcher conducts a study about establishing equity in South African higher education between Blacks and White Afrikaners (a person born, raised, or living in South Africa whose first language is Afrikaans and whose ancestors were Dutch). Let us further assume that the investigation is using a White female and Black female South African to illustrate the point. To apply the notion of social justice we just explained, we should consider how we decide on the calculus of social interest, how we rationalize when comparing the two individuals, and how do we address their backgrounds to arrive at an objective view of the current set of circumstances and their significance rather than attempting to unfold a complicated historical set of events that may not yield anything meaningful as result of the research. But before we proceed with our example, let us consider the role of the researcher.

The GRIID researcher is not merely a narrator of a story but is normally either immersed in it or somewhat connected to the problem, impacting the research outcome. Therefore, the GRIID researcher must (a) reconcile fairness and self-interest to objectively assess and evaluate the needs and input of the participants in a study, (b) be aware of the conceptual frame, the personal psychology, and one's social disposition that influence the reconciliation of fairness and self-interest, and (c) be cognizant that the reconciliation of fairness with self-interest is based on the relationship of the researcher as the observer, the allocator of meaning, and the rewardee making sense of the data presented by the study (van den Bos et al., 2015).

SCENARIO: THE ROLE OF THE RESEARCHER

As the researcher begins to investigate the South African Black female vs. the White South African female, the researcher must frame the problem in a way that each of the two females can be treated equitably without prejudice. The researcher must determine self-interest in the research and how biases can be eliminated or minimized to arrive at objective findings. Additionally, the researcher must determine what type of meaning the study is attempting to uncover, for what purpose, and how the findings would help advance social justice positively to help all stakeholders. Therefore, the investigation must consider how the conceptual frame will influence procedural justice in arriving at an objective view in allocating meaning correctly, leading to rewards for all stakeholders in the research. Finally, the researcher must review for adequacy of the context within which the research will be conducted. If there is adequate context, it is possible to pursue cause-and-effect investigation using a quantitative approach. However, lack of or inadequacy of context may lead to distortions of the cause and effect, and derail the intent of the study, leading to possible social injustice. Therefore, the researcher and the team undertaking a GRIID investigation must be mindful of the approach they take. We will expand on this issue in Chapters 5 and 6.

Törnblom and Vermunt (2007) addressed social justice as distributive and procedural simultaneously. Törnblom and Vermunt (2007) explained that to properly define social justice, one should view distributive and procedural justice in light of Stacy Adam's equity theory and Foa and Foa's resource theory. Törnblom and Vermunt argued that there is an isomorphic relationship between distributive and procedural justice, with resources and expectations impacting cognitive and affective outcomes. The overarching implication of the perspective of justice is that when research is conducted, the researcher's social disposition in terms of distributive or procedural justice and the researched subjects' in terms of equity and resources influence the research process.

Philosophically, due to our focus on social science research and the researcher, we will not address *restorative* and *criminal justice*, which deals with punishment as corrective measures, although they offer unique perspectives on procedural justice within different indigenous and national cultural settings (Braithwaite, 2006). We will focus on and define *procedural* and *distributive justice* to explain the nature of administration and disposition of social justice in the context of GRIID research.

Procedural justice

Procedural justice is the administration of justice by the institutions of a social system and may have to be subject to meritocratic administrative structure, an intolerable, yet favored over other systems incapable of dispensing justice fairly (Rawls, 2005). Procedural justice is also defined as "[t]he legal process and the imposition of proportionate punishment" (Nugent, 2013, para. 1).

Distributive justice

Frohlich (2007) traced the history of distributive justice to Plato and re-examined its history in light of four strands of thinking from Fleischacker's perspective, who considered reactionaries such as Malthus and Spencer, positivists, Marx, Utilitarian, and Rawls. Distributive justice as addressed by Rawls is not the contractarian view of the utilitarian application of justice but justice dispensed to all based on procedural justice when it is correctly formulated and implemented beyond deontological and teleological considerations (Rawls, 2005). As innovations change societies, the impact of innovations and their dynamic relationship with the ontology of social justice becomes a quandary requiring resolution (Abolhasani et al., 2014). In social sciences, the notion of distributive justice includes the individuals' thinking, intentions, and actions (Jasso, 2015). Distributive justice can be addressed from the etic perspective, global natural laws, or emic, specific sociocultural behaviors (Sabbagh & Golden, 2007). A variety of factors can influence the nature of distributive justice.

First, it is important to note that due to lack of a coherent unifying global moral view, the disposition of distributive justice requires disaggregation (de Bres, 2013). Second, distributive justice when examined psychologically, based on the "maximally unfair distribution (MUA)," presents individuals' perception and sensitivity about how resources are allocated (Eriksson, Kazemi, & Törnblom, 2015). Third, individual unconscious race biases result in distorted moral judgement and equity in distributive justice (Cameron, Payne, & Knobe, 2010). Fourth, psychodynamics, gestalt processes, self-identity, and self-defensive emotions such as fear, anger, bias influence the nature of distributive justice by different parties within the process (Turner, 2007).

SCENARIO: THE SITUATEDNESS

As the researcher begins examining the issues, the research should provide both emic and etic views of the situation requiring investigation. In our example about establishing equity in South African higher education between Black and White, rather than attempting to artificially conceptualize White vs. Black South African, perhaps the researcher should look deeper and provide a context for the complexity of the issue based on the situation today and its surroundings corollary to the problem. Several factors such as background to the characters under investigation and their social setting, their unique set of circumstances that may differentiate them from what the researcher may have determined based on a literature review, the spatiotemporal epitome approach to conducting the investigation, and how the research would provide social justice without further exasperating an uncontrollable social situation should be considered.

Justice, positivism, and objectivity

While the positivist focus is maintaining authority and structure, such as the Chicago School of Economics methodology maintaining the status quo of laissez faire (Wilber & Wisman, 1975), the dialogist focus is on creating ontology and epistemology underpinning their intended action to address social situations (Scollon, 2003). At the core of any GRIID inquiry resides the unconscious need for action with *a priori* understandings and categories of action (Gerstein, 1979). Therefore, any research attempting to address the disparities and proclivities has two choices: either ground the work in the world of nature or strictly adhere to a positivist approach, or social contract, as argued by Hobbes, Locke, and alike (Gerstein, 1979). The GRIID researcher must take note that at the center of positivism resides the need for intra-rater reliability with a single rater scoring consistently (Gallagher, 2014) assuming an etic view of reasons for actions and their causes. Regardless of the choice, with such approaches to inquiry, the researcher must be mindful that the outcomes can only provide the cues about the behavior and not the reason or the causes of any action. Therefore, positivism as a worldview and methodology would not lend itself to address social justice. Its etic view of behavior rests within the Western notion of psychometric statistical intra-reliability without concern for emic views that are different from the West. This etic view is demonstrated when explaining the roots of problems or even the reliability of instruments when applied to different sets of criteria embedded in temporal cultures that cannot be bounded by geography or unique national identities.

Positive social change

Positive social change can be surmised as any intellectual or physical activity empowering individuals to liberate their minds from the yoke of hegemonic systems and ideas to serve the well-being of others in their communities and societies, and call-to-action approaches, methods, and processes that enable others to benefit from equity and resources within the social systems in which they live in.

Various educational institutions have already undertaken positive social change as their mission to help build the intellectual capacity to address social justice and help their graduates formulate action plans for redressing equity. The following are a few examples. Oregon State University (2017) defines social change as the capacity "to enable individuals and communities to flourish." Walden University (2017) defines positive social change as "a deliberating process of creating and applying ideas, strategies, and actions to promote the worth, dignity, and development of individuals, communities, organizations, institutions, cultures, and societies." Saybrook University (2017) describes positive social change as "rigorous graduate education that inspires transformational change in individuals, organizations, and communities, toward a just, humane, and sustainable world." The University of Kwazulu-Natal (2017) explains its approach to positive social change as "A truly South African university that is academically excellent, innovative in research, critically engaged with society and demographically representative, redressing the disadvantages, inequities and imbalances of the past." Massey University (2018) describes its approach to positive social change: "Our mission is to work with and for communities to identify and enact innovative and responsive solutions to educational inequity." Although not exhaustive, the examples provide a window into a trend by higher education institutions that are attempting to address social justice by helping their researchers and graduates grasp the importance of the issue.

In light of the institutional efforts to help their researchers and graduates address social justice, one must ask the question of how that goal is set. What are its objectives and to what extent can researchers and graduates reconcile their own liberty with achieving justice for others, as the fundamental contradiction between Dewey's ideas and Rawls's continues (Weitz, 1993)? As GRIID researchers, ontologically and epistemologically, we have the responsibility to serve the interests of the research subjects to help improve lives based on our findings. Therefore, as researchers who are involved in the exploration of social issues, we must become familiar with the notion of social justice.

The core of the positivity

At the core of GRIID research rests the requirement for objectivity, mitigating bias, and leveling the playing fields. The researcher is responsible for objectivity when researching gender topics such as lesbian, gay, transsexual, queer, men, or women issues; race topics involving White, Black, or people of other races; identity topics by which an individual identifies and relates; indigeneity topics such as the interconnection of race, culture, and place (e.g., Māori in New Zealand, aboriginals in Australia, or Swahili across Uganda, Tanzania, and Kenya); or diversity topics such as the differences between ideas, race, or other factors.

Any researcher, whether a doctoral student or an occasional researcher, undertaking social science research must be cognizant of the findings' implications for society. It is imperative that researchers undertake meaningful studies that can improve the lives of the communities in which they operate. We believe that meaningful GRIID research must be rooted in social justice and the outcomes should provide a basis for positive social change. However, obstacles do exist.

There are numerous challenges in addressing social justice in creating positive social change. For example, others' perception of one's locus of control and power can distort one's intent to help with creating social justice. For example, in a meeting an organizer can be perceived as the boss controlling the process while the organizer simply intends to facilitate the process (Nygreen, 2009). Second, national culture may distort the nature and extent of equity and equality differently (Otto, Baumert, & Bobocel, 2011). Third, when addressing issues, an entire indigenous population may have been left out of the conversation, excluding them from social justice processes or excluding a topic to avoid conflict of interest by the researcher (Lawrence & Dua, 2005; Opotow, 1990). Therefore, the GRIID researcher must clarify the approach to the issue under investigation by explaining the research intent, how the results would be sought, and how the result would serve to create positive social change.

The researcher's approach

The researcher's approach in framing the investigation will create a set of assumptions about social justice and the research's results ontologically and epistemologically. In this chapter, we are only focused on social justice. We will address the ontological and epistemological assumption in Chapter 5. Here, we will address the issues that would influence the researcher's approach in respect to social justice.

1. A GRIID researcher, when he or she feels that his or her personal and social identity is not fairly perceived, has the motivation to find flaws and cast doubt on findings (Mayer et al., 2009). When a researcher treats participants with respect as an outsider to a group, this will increase the participants' positive perception of procedural justice by the research (Davies & Sivasubramaniam, 2016).
2. A GRIID researcher must overcome his or her deontic notion of justice and follow a research process that avoids the participant deontic ideals to remain objective in arriving at the results (O'Reilly, Aquino, & Skarlicki, 2016).
3. A GRIID researcher must pay attention to participants' group identification and how their participation in the research process may lead to sanctions that may distort their input (Cremer, Hoogervorst, & Desmet, 2012).
4. Justice (Moore, 2001), its role in GRIID research (Joyner, 2003; Markovsky & Younts, 2001), the underlying values and biases (Mayton, Ball-Rokeach, & Loges, 1994; Opotow, 2001; Rudman, 2004), and prior experiences (van den Bos et al., 2005) influence the researcher, the research participants, and the objectivity of the results.
5. Etic or emic positioning of GRIID research with its roots in psychology and history influences data collection and analysis (Culp, 2017; de Bres, 2013; Sabbagh & Golden, 2007; Perlman, Hunter, & Stewart, 2015).
6. When conducting GRIID research, ideological and psychological roots and processes and group/intergroup issues (Feygina, 2013; Marques & Paez, 1994) require dissection and clarification to contextualize the meaning of social justice.
7. There are a number of best practices in unfolding the meaning of social justice that can be applied when conducting GRIID research in general (Dietz, Kalof, & Stern, 2002; Fiske & Borgida, 2011), applied to

organizations (Harrison, & Klein, 2007; Klein & Harrison, 2007) and posing research questions (Okimoto, 2014).

8. The researcher must also take care to address social justice inferences (Ham & van den Bos, 2011; Jasso, 2007), avoid the advocacy role to maintain objective investigation (Levy et al., 2016), and integrate social justice in all phases of the research (Wagner, 2007; Törnblom, Jasso, & Vermunt, 2007).

The research intent

The research intent is intertwined with the researcher's objectivity and psychology in addressing social justice when researching GRIID. Multiple views offer different perspectives on explaining the researcher's frame of mind in meeting the research's intent. Frye (2016) argued that a researcher can be consumed with resentment, lack of self-respect created by unfavorable life experiences, the nature of social contract, and the motivation to create equality equilibrium when conducting research after an oppressive system has ended (e.g., after Apartheid ended in 1994 in South Africa). Stouten, Kuppens, and Decoster (2013)—using the five factors of personality inventory of neuroticism, extraversion, openness to experience, agreeableness, and conscientiousness (as explained by McCrae & Costa, 1991) and appraisal theory—postulated that when an individual, which for the purpose of our discussion would be a researcher, interacts with others where the principle of equality has been violated, he or she has the tendency to react with anger in restoring distributive justice. Lister (2013) provided a different perspective on the nature of psychological factors by explaining the relational factors influencing distributive justice universally independent of state construction of procedural infrastructure. Lister (2013) reasoned that an individual (i.e., the researcher) allows for equilibrium in a research intent rather than one dominated by anger through relationships rested in goals (creating a reciprocal benefit), ground (benefiting you because you benefited me), background conditions (sense of duty and expectations), and constraints (reciprocal conditions such as moral obligations). Therefore, as Lister viewed distributive justice, a researcher grounds his or her work in reciprocal relations rather than embedded in respect and recognition. However, other factors can influence the intent of GRIID research in addition to the researcher's psychology and relationships.

Several factors can change or skew the intent of GRIID research if the limitations of research are not clearly defined. For example, juxtaposition of emic or etic views can impact the intent of GRIID research. Otto, Baumert, and Bobocel (2011) claimed that etic views rely on tangibility of equity and equality, whereas emic views rest of intangible ideas of equity and equality, hence changing the nature of social justice dispensed as a result of particular research. As Eriksson, Kazemi, and Törnblom (2015) and Stouten, Cremer, and Dijk (2007) argued that social justice is dyadic: as one receives more, the other receives less. This counterbalancing principle is of importance in GRIID research. The researcher should be aware of the extent to which the research intends to offset the counter balance and to what end and how that intent is justified for the greater good. Matania and Yaniv (2007) posited that when research is focused on resource allocation, the dyadic nature of social justice will be tilted by economic efficiency rather than addressing inequities. Therefore, the researcher must be mindful of the research intent. If the purpose of research is to create more equal distribution of resources, then social justice can be appropriately served (Eriksson, Kazemi, & Törnblom, 2015; Matania & Yaniv, 2007). However, if the intent of research is to address equity among the oppressed categories of people, classes, casts, gender, and sex, then social justice dispensation requires more careful considerations by the researcher.

Distributive social justice rests on the idea of fairness in hearing voices. However, participants in a study, depending on the relevance of sociopsychological factors, may not be interested or want to air their voices (Platow et al., 2015), may have a different self-rumination process in assessing fairness (Brebels et al., 2013), may have different orientation depending on the organizational context where equality and diversity may be perceived differently by different participants based on reconciliation of different interests (Tomlinson & Schwabenland, 2010), and when conducting research involving indigenous population, the layers of reflexivity by respondents may provide a different context for fairness (Nicholls, 2009). Other challenges in remaining objective throughout the research by the researcher and participants include the idea of deservedness to some level of equity claimed (Smith, 2002), individuals' values, self-interest, and surrounding environment, including psychological (Dietz, Kalof, & Stern, 2002), and the level of group uniformity from which research participants are selected (Marques & Paez, 1994).

Summary

Any social research, particularly GRIID studies, should yield positive social outcomes addressing issues, problems, and situations that can improve human conditions. This chapter explained the role of social justice in conducting GRIID research and provided research scenarios illustrating the complexities and intersectionality of social justice and the research purpose.

EXERCISES

a   How would you explain the aim of achieving social justice in the literature review section of your work and balancing that with the need for objectivity in your methodology chapter?

b   There are times when an investigator might have psychologically or socially been subject to some sort of oppression as the result of individual or social actions and policies. Explain how your research can address both equity in creating positive social change based on your work's findings and objectivity in the process of your research, while as the investigator you have been subject to oppression by the status quo before the research was started?

References

Abolhasani, Z., Hassanzadeh, A., Ghazinoory, S. S., & Pourezzat, A. (2014). A justice-oriented innovation system: A grounded theory approach. *Social Justice Research*, 27(3), 369–394. doi:10.1007/s11211-014-0218-2

Berkey, B. (2016). Against Rawlsian Institutionalism about Justice. *Social Theory & Practice*, 42(4), 706–732. doi:10.5840/soctheorpract201642424

Bishop, R. (2005). Freeing Ourselves from Neocolonial Domination in Research: A Kaupapa Maori Approach to Creating Knowledge. In N. K. Denzin & Y. Lincoln (Eds.), *The Sage Handbook of Qualitative Research* (3rd ed., pp. 109–138). Thousand Oaks, CA: SAGE Publications.

Braithwaite, J. (2006). Doing Justice Intelligently in Civil Society. *Journal of Social Issues*, 62(2), 393–409.

Brebels, L., De Cremer, D., Sedikides, C., & Van Hiel, A. (2013). Self-focus and procedural fairness: The role of self-rumination and self-reflection. *Social Justice Research*, 26(2), 151–167. doi:10.1007/s11211-013-0180-4

Cameron, C., Payne, B., & Knobe, J. (2010). Do Theories of Implicit Race Bias Change Moral Judgments? *Social Justice Research*, 23(4), 272–289.

Colquitt, J. A., Long, D. M., Rodell, J. B., & Halvorsen-Ganepola, M. K. (2015). Adding the 'in' to justice: A qualitative and quantitative investigation of the differential effects of justice rule adherence and violation. *Journal of Applied Psychology*, 100(2), 278–297. doi:10.1037/a0038131

Cremer, D. D., Hoogervorst, N., & Desmet, P. (2012). Procedural justice and sanctions in social dilemmas: The moderating effects of group feedback and identification. *Journal of Applied Social Psychology*, 42(7), 1675–1693. doi:10.1111/j.1559-1816.2012.00914.x

Culp, J. (2017). Disaggregated pluralistic theories of global distributive justice—a critique. *Journal of Global Ethics*, 13(2), 168–186. doi:10.1080/17449626.2017.1371062

Davics, L., & Sivasubramaniam, D. (2016). Respectful inter-group interactions: A method for revising group attachment? *Social Justice Research*, 29(3), 288–309. doi:10.1007/s11211-016-0268-8

de Bres, H. (2013). Disaggregating Global Justice. *Social Theory & Practice*, 39(3), 422–448. doi:10.5840/soctheorpract201339324

Deutsch, M. (2006). A Framework for Thinking about Oppression and Its Change. *Social Justice Research*, 19(1), 7–41. doi:10.1007/s11211-006-9998-3

Dietz, T., Kalof, L., & Stern, P. C. (2002). Gender, Values, and Environmentalism. *Social Science Quarterly*, 83(1), 353–364. doi:10.1111/1540-6237.00088

Eriksson, K., Kazemi, A., & Törnblom, K. (2015). A new look at individual differences in perceptions of unfairness: The theory of maximally unfair allocations in multiparty situations. *Social Justice Research*, 28(4), 401–414. doi:10.1007/s11211-015-0255-5

Feygina, I. (2013). Social justice and the human–environment relationship: Common systemic, ideological, and psychological roots and processes. *Social Justice Research*, 26(3), 363–381. doi:10.1007/s11211-013-0189-8

Fine, M., & Weis, L. (2005). Compositional Studies, In Two Parts. In N. K. Denzin & Y. S. Lincoln (Eds.), *The Sage Handbook of Qualitative Research* (3rd ed., pp. 65–84). Thousand Oaks, CA: SAGE Publications.

Fiske, S. T., & Borgida, E. (2011). Best Practices: How to Evaluate Psychological Science for Use by Organizations. *Research in Organizational Behavior*, 31, 253–275.

Frohlich, N. (2007). A very short history of distributive justice. *Social Justice Research*, 20(2), 250–262. doi:10.1007/s11211-007-0039-7

Frye, H. P. (2016). The Relation of Envy to Distributive Justice. *Social Theory & Practice*, 42
(3), 501–524. doi:10.5840/soctheorpract201642314

Gallagher, C. W. (2014). Immodest Witnesses: Reliability and Writing Assessment. *Composition Studies*, 42(2), 73–95.

Gerstein, D. R. (1979). Durkheim and The Structure of Social Action. *Sociological Inquiry*, 49(1),
27–39.

Greenwood, D. J., & Levin, M. (2005). Reform of the Social Sciences and of Universities
through Action Research. In N. K. Denzin & Y. S. Lincoln (Eds.), *The Sage Handbook of
Qualitative Research* (3rd ed., pp. 53–64). Thousand Oaks, CA: SAGE Publications.

Ham, J., & van den Bos, K. (2011). On justice knowledge activation: Evidence for spontaneous activation of social justice inferences. *Social Justice Research*, 24(1), 43–65.
doi:10.1007/s11211-011-0123-x

Harrison, D. A., & Klein, K. J. (2007). What's the difference? Diversity constructs as separation,
variety, or disparity in organizations. *Academy of Management Review*, 32(4), 1199.

Jasso, G. (2007). Theoretical Unification in Justice and Beyond. *Social Justice Research*, 20(3),
336–371. doi:10.1007/s11211-007-0055-7

Jasso, G. (2015). Thinking, saying, doing in the world of distributive justice. *Social Justice
Research*, 28(4), 435–478. doi:10.1007/s11211-015-0257-3

Joyner, L. M. (2003). Applied Research in the Pursuit of Justice: Creating Change in the
Community and the Academy. *Social Justice*, 30(4), 5–20.

Klein, K. J., & Harrison, D. A. (2007). On the diversity of diversity: Tidy logic, messier
realities. *The Academy of Management Perspectives*, 21(4). 26.

Koirala-Azad, S., & Fuentes, E. (2009). Introduction: activist scholarship—possibilities and
constraints of participatory action research. *Social Justice*, 36(4), 1–5.

Lawrence, B., & Dua, E. (2005). Decolonizing antiracism. *Social Justice*, 32(4), 120.

Levy, S. R., Macdonald, J. L., Nelson, T. D., & Eagly, A. H. (2016). When Passionate
Advocates Meet Research on Diversity, Does the Honest Broker Stand a Chance? *Journal
of Social Issues*, 72(1), 199–222. doi:10.1111/josi.12163

Lister, A. (2013). Reciprocity, Relationships, and Distributive Justice. *Social Theory & Practice*,
39(1), 70–94. doi:10.5840/soctheorpract20133919

McCrae, R. R., & Costa, P. J. (1991). The NEO personality inventory: Using the five-factor model in counseling. *Journal of Counseling and Development*, 69(4), 367–372.

Mahoney, K. T. (2013). Equity Theory at 50. *TIP: The Industrial-Organizational Psychologist*,
51(2), 158.

Markovsky, B., & Younts, C. W. (2001). Prospects for Distributive Justice Theory. *Social
Justice Research*, 14(1), 45–59.

Marques, J. M., & Paez, D. (1994). The 'Black Sheep Effect': Social Categorization,
Rejection of Ingroup Deviates, and Perception of Group Variability. *European Review of
Social Psychology*, 5(1), 37. doi:10.1080/14792779543000011

Massey University. (2018). Vision/Mission. Retrieved from Massey University: www.ma
ssey.ac.nz/massey/learning/departments/centres-research/centre-excellence-research-in
clusive-education/our-mission.cfm

Matania, E., & Yaniv, I. (2007). Resource priority, fairness, and equality-efficiency compromises. *Social Justice Research*, 20(4), 497–510. doi:10.1007/s11211-007-0052-x

Mayer, D. M., Greenbaum, R. L., Shteynberg, G., & Kuenzi, M. (2009). When Do Fair
Procedures Not Matter? A Test of the Identity Violation Effect. *Journal of Applied Psychology*, 94(1), 142–161.

Mayton, D. I., Ball-Rokeach, S. J., & Loges, W. E. (1994). Human values and social issues:
An introduction. *Journal of Social Issues*, 50, 1–8. doi:10.1111/j.1540-4560.1994.tb01194.x

Moore, D. (2001). The Sense of Justice—Introduction. *Social Justice Research*, 14(3), 233–235.

Nicholls, R. (2009). Research and Indigenous participation: Critical reflexive methods. *International Journal of Social Research Methodology*, 12(2), 117–126.
Nugent, Pam M. S., 'JUSTICE' in PsychologyDictionary.org, 11 May 2013, https://p sychologydictionary.org/justice (accessed 21 July 2017).
Nygreen, K. (2009). Critical dilemmas in PAR: toward a new theory of engaged research for social change. *Social Justice*, 36(4), 14–35.
Okimoto, T. (2014). Toward More Interesting Research Questions: Problematizing Theory in Social Justice. *Social Justice Research* , 27(3), 395–411. doi:10.1007/s11211-014-0215-5
Opotow, S. (1990). Deterring Moral Exclusion. *Journal of Social Issues*, 46(1), 173–182.
Opotow, S. (2001). Reconciliation in Times of Impunity: Challenges for Social Justice. *Social Justice Research*, 14(2), 149–170.
Oregon State University. (2017). Positive Social Change. Retrieved from Oregon State University: http://sli.oregonstate.edu/feature-story/positive-social-change
O'Reilly, J., Aquino, K., & Skarlicki, D. (2016). The lives of others: Third parties' responses to others' injustice. *Journal of Applied Psychology*, 101(2), 171–189. doi:10.1037/apl0000040
Otto, K., Baumert, A., & Bobocel, R. D. (2011). Cross-cultural preferences for distributive justice principles: Resource type and uncertainty management. *Social Justice Research*, 24(3), 255–277. doi:10.1007/s11211-011-0135-6
Perlman, D., Hunter, A. G., & Stewart, A. J. (2015). Psychology, history, and social justice: Concluding reflections. *Journal of Social Issues*, 71(2), 402–413. doi:10.1111/josi.12118
Platow, M. J., Huo, Y. J., Lim, L., Tapper, H., & Tyler, T. R. (2015). Social identification predicts desires and expectations for voice. *Social Justice Research*, 28(4), 526–549. doi:10.1007/s11211-015-0254-6
Pollack, S., & Eldridge, T. (2016). Complicity and redemption: Beyond the insider/outsider research dichotomy. *Social Justice*, 42(2), 132.
Rawls, J. (2005). *A Theory of Justice*. Cambridge, MA: Harvard University Press.
Rudman, L. A. (2004). Social Justice in Our Minds, Homes, and Society: The Nature, Causes, and Consequences of Implicit Bias. *Social Justice Research*, 17(2), 129–142.
Sabbagh, C., & Golden, D. (2007). Reflecting upon etic and emic perspectives on distributive justice. *Social Justice Research*, 20(3), 372–387. doi:10.1007/s11211-007-0042-z
Saybrook University. (2017). Mission and Values. Retrieved from Saybrook University: www.saybrook.edu/about/essentials/mission-and-values
Scollon, R. (2003). The Dialogist in a Positivist World: Theory in the Social Sciences and the Humanities at the End of the Twentieth Century. *Social Semiotics*, 13(1), 71–88.
Smith, H. J. (2002). Review Essay: Thinking About Deservingness. *Social Justice Research*, 15(4), 409–422.
Smith, L. T. (2005). On Tricky Ground. In N. K. Denzin & Y. Lincoln (Eds.), *The Sage Handbook of Qualitative Research* (3rd ed., pp. 5–107). Thousand Oaks, CA: SAGE Publications.
Stouten, J., Cremer, D., & Dijk, E. (2007). Managing Equality in Social Dilemmas: Emotional and Retributive Implications. *Social Justice Research*, 20(1), 53–67. doi:10.1007/s11211-007-0032-1
Stouten, J., Kuppens, P., & Decoster, S. (2013). Being angry for different reasons: The role of personality in distributive justice. *Journal of Applied Social Psychology*, 43(4), 795–805. doi:10.1111/jasp.12005
Tomlinson, F., & Schwabenland, C. (2010). Reconciling competing discourses of diversity? The UK non-profit sector between social justice and the business case. *Organization*, 17(1), 101–121.
Törnblom, K., Jasso, G., & Vermunt, R. (2007). Theoretical integration and unification: A focus on justice. *Social Justice Research*, 20(3), 263–269. doi:10.1007/s11211-007-0044-x
Törnblom, K., & Vermunt, R. (2007). Towards an Integration of distributive justice, procedural justice, and social resource theories. *Social Justice Research*, 20(3), 312–335. doi:10.1007/s11211-007-0054-8

Turner, J. (2007). Justice and Emotions. *Social Justice Research*, 20(3), 288–311. doi:10.1007/s11211-007-0043-y

University of Kwazulu-Natal (2017). Vision & Mission. Retrevied from Kwazulu-Natal University: www.ukzn.ac.za/about-ukzn/vision-and-mission

van den Bos, K., Burrows, J. W., Umphress, E., Folger, R., Lavelle, J. J., Eaglestone, J., & Gee, J. (2005). Prior Experiences as Temporal Frames of Reference in Social Justice: The Influence of Previous Fairness Experiences on Reactions to New and Old Supervisors. *Social Justice Research*, 18(2), 99–120. doi:10.1007/s11211-005-7365-4

van den Bos, K., Cropanzano, R., Kirk, J., Jasso, G., & Okimoto, T. G. (2015). Expanding the horizons of social justice research: Three essays on justice theory. *Social Justice Research*, 28(2), 229–246. doi:10.1007/s11211-015-0237-7

Wagner, D. G. (2007). The limits of theoretical integration. *Social Justice Research*, 20(3), 270–287. doi:10.1007/s11211-007-0045-9

Walden University. (2017). Vision, Mission, and Goals. Retrieved from Walden University Catalogue: http://catalog.waldenu.edu/content.php?catoid=57&navoid=7946

Walster, E., & Walster, G. W. (1975). Equity and Social Justice. *Journal of Social Issues*, 31(3), 21–43.

Walter, M., & Anderson, C. (2013). *Indigenous Statistics: A Quantitative Research Methodology*. Walnut Creek, CA: Left Coast Press.

Weitz, B. A. (1993). Equality and justice in education: Dewey and Rawls. *Human Studies*, 16(4), 421–434.

Wilber, C. K., & Wisman, J. D. (1975). The Chicago School: Positivism or Ideal Type. *Journal of Economic Issues (Association for Evolutionary Economics)*, 9(4), 665.

Zapata-Sepulveda, P., Jara-Labarthe, V., & Espinoza-Verdejo, A. (2014). It All Depends on the Beholder: Decolonizing the Concept of Gender-Based Violence Against Aymara Women in Northern Chile. *Qualitative Inquiry*, 20(7), 928–933.

3

RESPONSIBLE RESEARCH

As social science researchers, we have a responsibility to navigate through the research process and observe a set of complex ethical rules. Protecting the rights of research participants, maintaining objectivity, understanding the effects of procedural and distributive social justice on the research and emanating from the research, and understanding the impact of a researcher's ontological and epistemological perspectives in creating knowledge are among the ethical challenges that a social science researcher must address. For a doctoral student conducting gender, race, identity, indigeneity, and diversity (GRIID) studies, the stated issues must be explained in a number of different ways and to different people and entities. Although GRIID can expand across multiple disciplines such as psychology, sociology, management, leadership, business, anthropology, just to name a few, and each discipline may have slight variations in its approach to observing ethical rules, there are fundamental common themes that we will address in this chapter.

In this chapter, we will define a researcher's ethics, explain the implications of academic imperialism, and address the role, requirements, and academic politics of an institutional review board (IRB), which may be referred to by other names such as research ethics board (REB), ethical review board (ERB), or independent ethics committee. As a part of the IRB process, we discuss the importance of protecting the participants' human rights and provide some scenarios based on the advanced arguments in the literature. We will also shed light on the impact of the researcher's orientation, the purpose of the research, and influence of dominant and marginalized academic theoretical and conceptual voices in GRIID research.

The researcher's ethics

Fundamentally, as individual researchers any endeavor we undertake has ethical implications. The implication of our research ethics is rooted in our psyche and perhaps deep within our subconscious. The way we arrive at the *aha* moment in noticing a problem, the way we state the problem, the method we use to address it, and the nature of our analysis even in quantitative studies are subject to our individual way of thinking, reflecting our identity (see our discussions in Chapter 2) as individuals and in relation to others and our environment. With the passage of time, our identity as related to others and the environment is influenced by the development of epistemology.

Within the last half century, developments in how knowledge is generated and acquired, social changes due to technological innovations (Krasner, 1965), the amassing of data in data warehouses (Sawyer & Schechter, 1968), and apprehension about unequal distributed power impacting the relationship between the powerful and the socially powerless (Barnes, 2016) have given rise to more stringent ethical requirements for conducting GRIID research across multiple disciplines. However, before addressing how research ethics should be observed, we should explain what we mean by ethics. Kant (2012a) stated:

> Ethical lawgiving (even if the duties might be external) is that which *cannot* be external; juridical lawgiving is that which can also be external. So, it is an external duty to keep a promise made in a contract; but the command to do this merely because it is a duty, without regard for any other incentive, belongs to *internal* lawgiving alone.
>
> *(p. 21)*

Kant (2012b) defined the external lawgiving as "the end of pure reason" (p. 38) and explained the internal lawgiving as the manifestation of man as a moral being "obligated to himself to be truthful" (p. 91). Empirical research, quantitative or qualitative, is subject to normativity of moral judgement yet is bound by the practice of pure reason, at a minimum by its utilitarianism, as argued by Rawls (Besser-Jones, 2012; Copp & Sobel, 2002; de Lazari-Radek & Singer, 2012; Kahane, 2014). The social science researcher (e.g., the GRIID researcher) at the center of it all has the responsibility to arrive at outcome beyond antinomy of determinism and free-will (Wallerstein, 1997). Therefore, GRIID researchers must clearly state their position ethically and morally to provide a clear link to their premise for conducting research while avoiding academic imperialism.

Avoiding academic imperialism

While we will address academic imperialism and its consequences for the GRIID researchers' ontological position and their epistemologies in Chapter 4, here we will address the ethical implication of academic imperialism. We define *academic imperialism* as the hegemonic position of perspectives based on a particular language usage and its associated psychological, sociopolitical, and economic implications in creating knowledge, marginalizing non-Western voices including indigenous and gender, race, and ethnic minorities living in Western countries. As such, several elements have contributed to academic imperialism; among the most critical are colonization, globalization, and expansion of digital media requiring uniformity and pervasive Eurocentricism in the face of decolonization and its associated new colonial educational research practices (Brannelly & Boulton, 2017; Habashi, 2005; Meyer, 2007; Popova & Beavitt, 2017; Wallace & Sheldon, 2015). To better acquaint our readers with the concept of academic imperialism and how to avoid it, we will take a detour by first explaining the importance of addressing this issue and introducing some literary and political work examining its roots and its evolution, before reviewing the possibilities to overcome it.

Postcolonialism can creep into any area of GRIID research in any discipline. Postcolonialism theories began emerging in the middle of the twentieth century as many countries in Africa, Asia, Americas, and the Pacific were decolonized. Colonialism reflected domination of many African and Asian countries by the Western powers. The colonization process, which took over 400 years to develop, was coming to an end in the mid-1950s. During 400 years of colonialization, two parallel sets of events took place: (a) in the West, natural sciences were developing exponentially while emerging philosophical views were pushing societies toward secularization and distribution of political power for their citizens, and (b) the colonies were forced to abandon their autochthonous identities, language, and traditions and be subjected to dominant powers ruling over them. Despite decolonization, colonial rule remained with a mask of postcolonial label. Postcolonialism resulted in two sets of circumstances: (a) countries such as Canada or Australia being ruled by the immigrants of the Western countries, and (b) countries where the Western powers withdrew their physical presence but left behind the means of thinking such as language and the way thoughts are communicated. While, in the former case, the indigenous population, their identity, their way of life, and their voices were marginalized, the latter also lost the ability to govern itself. At the core of postcolonialism remained the loss of identity, voices, and relationships.

Said (1979/1994) in his literary work observed that U.S. political dynamics combined with the European scientific positivist vision of the world have created a neocolonial reality extending the life of colonialism in Asia and Africa, present in every aspect of life and impacting academic voices. Philosophically, neocolonialism has been repackaged as postcolonialism, confusing some as to its ontological and epistemological meaning (Gandhi, 1998). When conducting GRIID research, postcolonialism views have ethical implications for neutrality and objectivity. Postcolonialism infers a temporal stage beyond colonialism. In this context, postcolonialism is defined as hegemonic social, political, and economic status that is enforced, articulated, and perpetuated through Western powers subjugating less powerful military geographical areas to their rules; yet it has been used by many in the last 30 years as signifying the ontological and epistemological appropriateness of this framework for investigating management and business practices (Prasad, Pisani, & Prasad, 2008; Dar, 2014).

Postcolonialism does not represent an opposing view to the colonial framework; it is rooted in it (Calas & Smirich, 1999). Postcolonialism imposes the colonial languages on societies including in the West (e.g., New Zealand, the United States) where there are indigenous populations and minorities (Makoni, Dube, & Mashiri,

2006) to articulate its views; its power structure is rooted in the colonialists' history represented by colonial/postcolonial periods (McLennan, 2014). Collier (2009) reasoned that societies such as those dominated by colonialists would always be subjugated to the rule of colonial masters due to a knowledge–power relationship framework. In this context, the colonial framework explains postcolonial inadequacies because it ignores identity (William, 2009) in GRIID research. Additionally, a postcolonial framework skews objectivity in pedagogy (Paschyn, 2014) examining GRIID and creates a binary model masking the colonial characteristics (Seremani & Clegg, 2016). When researching GRIID, a postcolonial framework leads to confusion about the language used between the researcher and the research participants in unfolding the meaning of GRIID in local contexts (Vambe & Rwafa, 2011). Therefore, postcolonial theories have several ethical implications for a GRIID researcher.

To ethically conduct research, the researcher should be free of the periodization (Friedman, 2006) to examine the object of inquiry critically (Tyson, 1999), and, when required, construct the phenomenon under consideration socially to contextualize the research (Özkazanc-Pan, 2008). Yet the researcher should be mindful of the created reality, self-perception, perception projected by the research subjects (Anderson, 1990; Merleau-Ponty, 1964), and language as mediating factors (Fashina, 2009) when conducting GRIID investigations. Regardless of qualitative or quantitative methodological use, GRIID research should be free from bias and provide adequate objectivity in cementing validity. In qualitative studies where questions are empirically unanswerable, meaning created through design and instruments should yield new theories (Maxwell, 1996), answering social justice concerns. In quantitative methods, as the research questions and hypothesis are formulated, the questions should present an adequate level of objectivity and neutrality (Huff, 2009), neither of which is possessed by postcolonialism.

Additionally, ethical consideration requires that the research subjects have a free voice to objectively state the reality as perceived by them, enabling the researcher to become intimately aware of what is being examined (Kamenou, 2007). Finally, language plays a mediating factor in communicating reality (Widding, 2012) and should be carefully reflected in the research design and research instruments to allow the research subject to express his or her perceived reality freely.

Languages communicate ideas existentially, influencing theoretical frameworks and actions. Postcolonialism possesses its own language embedded in colonialism, communicated by Westward-looking individuals who have illusively found space not in time but a third place or *Third World* (Trivedi, 1999; Bolton & Hutton, 2000). Postcolonial language, manifested in literary works, is demonstrative of the commoditization of cultural effects of the colonized, marginalizing local languages as irrelevant to history and perceptions of reality (Bolton & Hutton, 2000; Eze, 2008; Fashina, 2009; Garnier 2012). Therefore, freedom from postcolonialism is required to remain ethically transparent in explaining the emerging meaning or testing the relationships.

Postcolonialism can be ever-present in any GRIID research; for example, the way one undertakes studies of indigenous population, examining sexual or gender identity within a social context, selection of method to conduct research, or the process by which views of participants are examined. For example, when one conducts research involving an indigenous population, a researcher must address the way assessments are conducted, the nature of participants' trust in the researcher, the methodology, and the intended outcome with respect to social justice, which are a cornerstone of ethical considerations in the process (Kovach, 2018; Smith, 2005) and a way of avoiding postcolonial traps. Mortensen and Kirsch (1996) argued that the way to liberate researchers from academic imperialism is to allow them to have a footing in post-modernism ontologically and tell their own stories, defying the Eurocentric positivism epistemologically.

Ethics in the research process

As explained by Creswell (2014) and Patton (2002, 2015), there are general require-ments that a researcher must follow in meeting IRB approval before any investigation can begin. Alluded to by Bickman and Rog (1998), in social sciences IRB require-ments have stringent criteria for meeting the standards for the nature of observation and engaging the participants in the research process. In GRIID research, the IRB process focuses its attention on respect, beneficence, trust, and justice prominently (Denzin and Lincoln, 2005, 2018). Although different factors affect the ethical con-sideration, we will first examine the effects of the research type and the IRB process.

Research studies can be clinical, practice-based, or theoretical, each subject to the country's rules that govern the research ethics requirements and processes where the research is conducted. All states, regardless of variation in policies, adhere to the five general principles as outlined by the American Psychological Association (2018): (1) beneficence and non-maleficence, (2) fidelity and responsibility, (3) integrity, (4) jus-tice, and (5) respect for people's rights and dignity. Each of the five requirements may impact research differently, depending on the focus of the study on clinical trials, practice, or theory. For example, beneficence will be a primary ethical concern in ensuring that the outcome benefits far outweigh the possible harm and that partici-pants are fully aware of the risks. In GRIID studies, in addition to the requirements of the five general principles, other ethical issues also require addressing.

On a granular level, GRIID studies' ethical consideration involves authorship, the nature of the relationship with research participants, deontological ethics, and the ontological position of the author (Denzin & Lincoln, 2005, 2018; American Psy-chological Association, 2017, pp. 11, 20, 40, 231). A GRIID researcher should address these ethical issues at the inception of the work when the problem statement is for-mulated. We will address the ethical issues discussed as part of the participants' rights, the ethical choices that research makes within the context of the study, and the way research is ontologically positioned.

The research orientation: ethical choices

Researchers' orientation may be found in the background to a study, where they attempt to state a position, a lead-in to a problem statement, or in the purpose and the nature of the study. In either case, the researcher cognitively attempts to construct reality through an agreed-upon language medium, projecting how reality is perceived in physical, social, and temporal terms (Lincoln & Guba, 1985). Constructing reality in social sciences in general, and particularly in GRIID studies, contains several elements that determine the ethical choices a researcher makes. One such choice is the researcher's orientation in the construction of reality.

The cornerstone of Berger and Luckmann's approach to the construction of reality (as cited in Barnes, 2016) is that humans are born with a predisposition to sociality, they are interacting knowledge carriers, and knowledge is created collectively. Unlike others, Berger and Luckman provided a sociological theory of knowledge, connecting construction of reality as collective activity, posing a sociopolitical structure on a research outcome based on the way knowledge is created (Barnes, 2016; Dreher, 2016), which suggests that a researcher's findings are based on the shared collective reality; hence, a researcher's findings are not subject to an ethical perspective but rather the objective collective interaction. However, the need for self-interest when categorized within multiple minority groups can develop individual preferences in constructing social reality (Gaffié, Marchand, & Cassagne, 1997; Maass, Clark, & Haberkorn, 1982); thus, researchers are not immune to such biases in making ethical choices in finding their path to studies. Institutions of higher education are subject to policies driven by the public political will diminishing the freedom of research (Hoover & Howard, 1995). Therefore, regardless of political influence, socially, or through public policies impacting higher learning institutions, individual researchers take positions that have ethical consequences for the research outcome that should be noted as a limitation in studies. As Luhmann argued (as cited in Vermeer, 2006), the individual consciousness and social systems are autopoietic, and each is self-containing. Luhmann's argument rejects the ontological basis of collective consciousness and explains the reality of social system as independent of individuals' perception of it. Thus, declaring an ethical position is the researcher's responsibility in explaining the limitations and delimitations of studies.

When a researcher decides to investigate a problem, an ethical decision is made to advance the knowledge of theory or practice in a certain way. Therefore, the researcher is bound to explain the rationale for the decision. Regardless of social constraints, public policies, and dominant political ideologies, a researcher has the ultimate responsibility to determine objectivity and adhere to the five general research principles (American Psychological Association, 2018).

SCENARIO

Hook (2011) in his attempt to critique the misguided nature of racism in post-Apartheid South Africa began his paper by providing a context for his own ethical approach, informing the reader of the challenges of a White person examining racism from another's perspective. Throughout the paper, he made the reader aware of how one's internalized value systems can be manifested in so-called objectivity. He outlined the required disclosures to address his own ethics in solving the problems. However, the author is only one part of the ethical challenges in research.

The other part of the challenge is explicating the ethical consequences of the epistemology of a topic and its temporal positioning. For example, as Posel (2015) explained in an editorial, post-Apartheid South Africa was based on non-racialism, which is philosophically an ambiguous term and does not provide an objective definition of what is meant by it. As Posel (2015) suggested, in such cases where there is no clear definition, research ethics can be clouded by other actions (e.g., the Employment Equity Act in South Africa that appears to be contrapuntal to the notion of non-racialism, thus creating an ethical concern when addressing non-racialism in South Africa). Such an epistemological, ethical quandary becomes a flash point in researching the topic objectively (Posel, 2010; Whitehead, 2012).

As this writing scenario suggested, a researcher must clearly explain personal biases by divulging the underlying ethical assumption before starting the investigation and the ethical issues are interwoven into the epistemology of the topic. We will expand on how a researcher's ethical position should be clarified in a study as we move through Chapters 5 and 6.

The research process and ethics

Any doctoral research requires the formulation of a proposal containing three chapters before submitting for study approval by the IRB. Chapter 1 includes an introduction to the study to include the problem statement, purpose, research questions, the nature of the study, and its scope and limitations. Chapter 2 is dedicated to literature review, providing a historical evolution of the topic under consideration, explaining its breadth, the literature gap or practical problem based on the program orientation, and delineating the theoretical and conceptual underpinnings of the research. Chapter 3 is a methodological explanation of the research process, instruments, reliability, and validity. In each of the three chapters, the researcher must take the opportunity to clarify his/her ethical position with respect to the investigation that is about to start.

In qualitative studies, GRIID researchers must ethically ground the study. In the background to the study, the interwoven social justice challenges must be explained. In the theoretical foundation, the relevance of social justice as a way of explaining ethical concerns should be explicated, and in the conceptual framework the researcher's ethical intent as part of his or her worldview must be described. In the assumptions, scopes, and limitations, the author must explain how his or her worldview has ethical implications. Finally, in the significance section, the researcher must explain how social

TABLE 3.1 Chapter 3 sample layout

Qualitative	Quantitative
1. Introduction to the Study	1. Introduction to the Study/problem/
2. Background of the Study	context
3. Problem Statement	2. Purpose of the Study
4. Purpose of the Study	3. Research Question, Objectives,
5. Research Question	Hypotheses
6. Theoretical Foundation	4. Theoretical Perspectives
7. Conceptual Framework/Author's	5. Conceptual Framework/Author's
worldview	worldview
8. Nature of the Study	6. Definitions
9. Definitions	7. Assumptions, Scope, and limitations
10. Assumptions, Scope, and limitations	8. Significance
11. Significance	9. Summary & Transition
12. Summary & Transition	

Source: Fictitious data, for illustration purposes only

justice will be served by completing the research. In quantitative studies, social justice ramifications must be clarified when providing context. In the theoretical, conceptual, scope, limitations, and significance sections, a similar explanation must be provided in the qualitative studies.

In Chapter 2 of both qualitative and quantitative studies, GRIID researchers explaining the theme of the study must provide the relevant literature to social justice and its ethical consideration.

In qualitative studies, the researcher must clearly explain the ethical considerations and associated social justice ramifications in the researcher's role and the reason for conducting the study. In quantitative studies, the researcher must explicate the ethical concerns in the research design and context and their impact on social justice. Other critical ethical concerns in conducting GRIID studies include avoiding academic imperialism and attention for the human rights of study participants, which we will address next. Perhaps the most pertinent ethical consideration is the role of participants in the research process and how different GRIID research may require concise description of the nature of participants' involvement and how the researcher will shield them from harm.

TABLE 3.2 Chapter 2 sample layout

Qualitative	Quantitative
1. Literature Review Strategy	1. Literature Review Strategy
2. Theoretical Foundation	2. Theoretical Explanation
3. Conceptual Framework/Author's	3. Literature Review
worldview	4. Summary & Transition
4. Literature Review	
5. Summary & Transition	

Source: Fictitious data, for illustration purposes only

The human rights of participants

Regardless of a study's methodology, GRIID researchers must address the ethics of participants' selection and their rights. Although there are common ethical principles such as beneficence and justice that the researcher must consider, there are other elements that require attention based on methodologies. There are distinct ethical issues that must be addressed by a researcher in qualitative studies as opposed to the experimental and quantitative research.

We will first address the ethical concerns in participant selection in experimental and quantitative studies, although the idea may also be applicable to qualitative studies. First, a GRIID researcher must be cognizant that participants' rights are subject to IRBs' minimum requirements, known as the floor standard, subject to changes in social norms, technology, and the context (Cooper & McNair, 2017). Therefore, a doctoral researcher must be prepared to adequately explain how the participants' human rights would be protected through the process and as the result of the anticipated findings. For example, if the study is conducted on a dimension of gender issues in a country such as Saudi Arabia, how would the participants' anonymity be protected through the research process and after the research is completed to avoid legal prosecution?

Second, in GRIID research, doctoral students, based on their discipline and the methodology, must be concerned about the reproducibility and replicability of the process and findings, lack of which may lead to negative results for the participants (Redman & Caplan, 2016). For example, let us assume that we are to conduct quantitative research using some form of survey instrument that has been validated in a Western country to address the needs of Biharis, the stranded Pakistanis in Bangladesh. In this example, as a GRIID researcher we must explain why we think that the validated Western instrument is be able to help us conduct a replicable and valid outcome when the instrument would be applied within a different socio-economic context; examining a marginalized and persecuted minority within it, when even the official data may be a suspect and would not allow for cross-referencing with a secondary set of data. As we discussed in Chapter 2, cultural studies, such as those conducted by Hofstede, have assumptions beyond positivism to make the instruments applicable to examining cultural dimensions, relying on national cultures bound by geographic boundaries. An effective GRIID researcher would question assumptions such as those by Hofstede when addressing particularities of Biharis in Bangladesh, Swahilis across Kenya and Tanzania, aboriginals in Australia, or similar marginalized groups where culture becomes like the unbounded waters of the ocean, only allowing some things to float on the surface while other details are hidden or blended together.

Third, the researcher must clarify any undue influence on the research process and outcomes, such as the nature of benefits/harms to the participants, protecting the privacy of participants, any inducements for the participation and the rationale for their inclusion, the idiosyncratic nature of participants impacting the outcome, and the possible symbiotic idiosyncratic problems of the researcher and the participants that may taint the outcome (Largent & Fernandez Lynch, 2017). Although some have warned about undue influence in GRIID research based on the incentives provided to the participants, perhaps the nature of the researcher's relationship and interest of the researcher to the research subject is a *sine qua non*, presenting the most fundamental challenge to ethical consideration (Christians, 2018) and requiring transparency when submitting the paperwork to IRB and when soliciting participants and communicating with them.

Fourth, when considering inclusion of participants, the direct and indirect nature of coercive approaches to soliciting participation or subjugating marginalized and disadvantage voices by anyone should be addressed (Resnik, 2016; Singleton, Jones, & Hanumantha, 2014). In qualitative studies how do we arrive at selecting participants? For what purpose (Reybold, Lammert, & Stribling, 2013)?

Summary

Multiple factors influence the research ethics. Language, worldview, experiences, and other subconscious thoughts can change the nature of our data collection and analysis, taking findings in a different direction. This chapter explained factors such as our perspectives, the communities within which we live, our experiences, and similar factors involved in the GRIID research process impacting research ethics and how we should mitigate them.

EXERCISES

a   Review Indiana University IRB (https://research.iu.edu/forms/human-sub jects-irb.html) and University of Pretoria Research Ethics Committee (www. up.ac.za/healthethics), and identify the differences between the national and specific institutional requirements for research ethics.

b   Based on the differences found in the institutional requirements in the United States and South Africa, what ethical issues should be clearly explained and incorporated into a dissertation to have an acceptable etic rather than emic research position?

Exercises: link to https://research.iu.edu/forms/human-subjects-irb.html (Indiana University IRB), www.up.ac.za/healthethics (University of Pretoria Research Ethics Committee), and www.vu.edu.au/researchers/research-lifecycle/con ducting-research/human-research-ethics (Victoria University, Melbourne, Australia, Human Research Ethics)

References

American Psychological Association (2017). *Publication Manual of the American Psychological Association* (6th ed.). Washington, DC:American Psychological Association.

American Psychological Association (2018). *Ethical Principles of Psychologists and Code of Conduct.* Retrieved from www.apa.org/ethics/code/index.aspx

Anderson, W. (1990). *Reality Isn't What It Used to Be: Theatrical Politics, Ready-to-Wear Religion, Global Myths, Primitive Chic, and Other Wonders of the Postmodern World.* San Francisco: Harper & Row.

Barnes, B. (2016). On the Social Construction of Reality: Reflections on a Missed Opportunity. *Human Studies*, 39(1), 113–125. doi:10.1007/s10746-016-9389-1

Besser-Jones, L. (2012). The Role of Practical Reason in an Empirically Informed Moral Theory. *Ethical Theory & Moral Practice*, 15(2), 203–220. doi:10.1007/s10677-011-9284-9

Bickman, L., & Rog, D. J. (1998). *Handbook of Applied Social Research Methods.* Thousand Oaks, CA: SAGE Publications.

Bolton, K., & Hutton, C. (2000). Orientalism, Linguistics and Postcolonial Studies. *Interventions: The International Journal of Postcolonial Studies*, 2(1), 1–5.

Brannelly, T., & Boulton, A. (2017). The ethics of care and transformational research practices in Aotearoa New Zealand. *Qualitative Research*, 17(3), 340–350.

Calas, M. B. & Smircich, L. (1999). Past Postmodernism? Reflections and Tentative Directions. *Academy of Management Review*, 24(4), 649–671.

Christians, C. G. (2018). Ethics and Politics in Qualitative Research. In N. K. Denzin & Y. S. Lincoln (Eds.), *The Sage Handbook of Qualitative Research* (5th ed., pp. 66–82). Los Angeles: SAGE Publications.

Collier, S. J. (2009). Topologies of power Foucault's analysis of political government beyond 'governmentality'. *Theory, Culture & Society*, 26(6), 78–108.

Cooper, J. A., & McNair, L. (2017). Are the criteria for approval sufficient to protect research participants? *Journal of Empirical Research on Human Research Ethics*, 12(5), 383–385. doi:10.1177/1556264617737915

Copp, D., & Sobel, D. (2002). Desires, Motives, and Reasons: Scanlon's Rationalistic Moral Psychology. *Social Theory & Practice*, 28(2), 243–276.

Creswell, J. W. (2014). *Research Design: Qualitative, Quantitative, and Mixed Methods Approaches* (4th ed.). Thousand Oaks, CA: SAGE Publications.

Dar, S. (2014). Hybrid Accountabilities: When Western and Non-Western Accountabilities Collide. *Human Relations*, 67(2), 131–151.

de Lazari-Radek, K., & Singer, P. (2012). The Objectivity of Ethics and the Unity of Practical Reason. *Ethics*, 123(1), 9–31.

Denzin, N. K., & Lincoln, Y. S. (2005). *The SAGE Handbook of Qualitative Research* (3rd ed.). Thousand Oaks, CA: SAGE Publications.

Denzin, N. K., & Lincoln, Y. S. (2018). *The Sage Handbook of Qualitative Research* (5th ed.). Los Angeles, CA: SAGE Publications.

Dreher, J. (2016). The Social Construction of Power: Reflections beyond Berger/Luckmann and Bourdieu. *Cultural Sociology*, 10(1), 53–68.

Eze, E. C. (2008). Language and Time in Postcolonial Experience. *Research in African Literatures*, 39(1), 24–47.

Fashina, N. O. (2009). Alienation and Revolutionary Vision in East African Post-Colonial Dramatic Literature. *Ufahamu: A Journal of African Studies*, 35(2). Retrieved from: http://escholarship.org/uc/item/63k8d46k

Friedman, S. S. (2006). Periodizing Modernism: Postcolonial Modernities and the Space! Time Borders of Modernist Studies. *Modernism/Modernity*, 13(3), 425–443.

Gaffié, B., Marchand, P., & Cassagne, J. (1997). Effect of political position on group perception. *European Journal of Social Psychology*, 27(2), 177–187.

Gandhi, L. (1998). *Postcolonial Theory: A Critical Introduction.* New York: Columbia University Press.

Garnier, X. (2012). African-Language Literature; or, Postcolonial Theory's Unconscious. *Comparative Studies of South Asia, Africa and The Middle East*, 32(3), 502–510.

Habashi, J. (2005). Creating indigenous discourse: History, power, and imperialism in academia, Palestinian case. *Qualitative Inquiry*, 11(5), 771–788.

Hook, D. (2011). Retrieving Biko: a Black Consciousness critique of whiteness. *African Identities*, 9(1), 19–32. doi:10.1080/14725843.2011.530442

Hoover, J. D., & Howard, L. A. (1995). The political correctness controversy revisited. *American Behavioral Scientist*, 38(7), 963–975.

Huff, A. S. (2009). *Designing Research for Publication*. Thousand Oaks, CA: SAGE Publications.

Kahane, G. (2014). Evolution and Impartiality. *Ethics*, 124(2), 327–341.

Kamenou, N. (2007). Methodological considerations in conducting research across gender, 'race', ethnicity and culture: a challenge to context specificity in diversity research methods. *International Journal of Human Resource Management*, 18(11), 1995–2010.

Kant, I. (2012a). *The Metaphysics of Morals* (M. Gregor, Trans.). Cambridge: Cambridge University Press. (3rd print)

Kant, I. (2012b). *Groundwork of the Metaphysics of Morals* (rev. ed.) (M. J. Gregor, Ed.). Cambridge: Cambridge University Press.

Kovach, M. (2018). Doing Indigenous Methodologies: A Letter to a Research Class. In N. K. Denzin & Y. S. Lincoln (Eds.), *The Sage Handbook of Qualitative Research* (5th ed., pp. 214–234). Los Angeles, CA: SAGE Publications.

Krasner, L. (1965). The Behavioral Scientist and Social Responsibility: No Place to Hide. *Journal of Social Issues*, 21(2), 9–30.

Largent, E., & Fernandez Lynch, H. (2017). Paying Research Participants: The Outsized Influence of 'Undue Influence'. (Cover story). *IRB: Ethics & Human Research*, 39(4), 1–9.

Lincoln, Y. S., & Guba, E. G. (1985). *Naturalistic Inquiry*. Beverly Hills, CA: SAGE Publications.

Maass, A., ClarkIII, R. D., & Haberkorn, G. (1982). The effects of differential ascribed category membership and norms on minority influence. *European Journal of Social Psychology*, 12(1), 89–104.

McLennan, G. (2014). Complicity, complexity, historicism: Problems of postcolonial sociology. *Postcolonial Studies*, 17(4), 451–464. doi:10.1080/13688790.2014.966421

Makoni, S. B., Dube, B., & Mashiri, P. (2006). Zimbabwe Colonial and Post-Colonial Language Policy and Planning Practices. *Current Issues in Language Planning*, 7(4), 377–414. doi:10.2167/cilp108.0

Maxwell, J. A. (1996). *Qualitative Research Design: An Interactive Approach*. Thousand Oaks, CA: SAGE Publications.

Merleau-Ponty, M. (1964). *The Primacy of Perception: And Other Essays on Phenomenological Psychology, the Philosophy of Art, History, and Politics*. Evanston, IL: Northwestern University Press.

Meyer, H. (2007). Contorted Culture. The Price of Durkheim's Intellectual Imperialism. *Conference Papers—American Sociological Association*, 1–20.

Mortensen, P., & Kirsch, G. E. (1996). *Ethics and Representation in Qualitative Studies of Literacy*. Urbana, IL: National Council of Teachers of English.

Özkazanc-Pan, B. (2008). International management research meets the 'rest of the world'. *Academy of Management Review*, 33(4), 964–974. doi:10.5465/AMR.2008.34422014

Patton, M. Q. (2002). *Qualitative Research and Evaluation Methods* (3rd ed.). Thousand Oaks, CA: SAGE Publications.

Patton, M. Q. (2015). *Qualitative Research and Evaluation Methods: Integrating Theory and Practice* (4th ed.). Thousand Oaks, CA: SAGE Publications.

Paschyn, C. (2014). Check Your Orientalism at the Door: Edward Said, Sanjay Seth, and the Adequacy of Western Pedagogy. *Journal of General Education*, 63(2–3), 222–231.

Popova, N. G., & Beavitt, T. A. (2017). English as a Means of Scientific Communication: Linguistic Imperialism or Interlingua? *Integration of Education*, 21(1), 54–70. doi:10.15507/1991-9468.086.021.201701.054-070

Posel, D. (2010). Races to consume: Revisiting South Africa's history of race, consumption and the struggle for freedom. *Ethnic & Racial Studies*, 33(2), 157–175. doi:10.1080/01419870903428505

Posel, D. (2015). Whither 'non-racialism': The 'new' South Africa turns twenty-one. *Ethnic & Racial Studies*, 38(13), 2167–2174. doi:10.1080/01419870.2015.1058511

Prasad, S., Pisani, M., & Prasad, R. (2008). New criticisms of international management: An analytical review. *International Business Review*, 17(6), 617–629.

Redman, B. K., & Caplan, A. L. (2016). Limited reproducibility of research findings: Implications for the welfare of research participants and considerations for institutional review boards. *IRB: Ethics & Human Research*, 38(4), 8–10.

Resnik, D. B. (2016). Employees as research participants: Ethical and policy issues. *IRB: Ethics & Human Research*, 38(4), 11–16.

Reybold, L. E., Lammert, J. D., & Stribling, S. M. (2013). Participant selection as a conscious research method: Thinking forward and the deliberation of 'emergent' findings. *Qualitative Research*, 13(6), 699–716. doi:10.1177/1468794112465634

Said, E. W. (1979/1994). *Orientalism*. New York, NY: Vintage Books.

Sawyer, J., & Schechter, H. (1968). Computers, privacy, and the national data center: The responsibility of social scientists. *American Psychologist*, 23(11), 810–818. doi:10.1037/h0026719

Seremani, T. W., & Clegg, S. (2016). Postcolonialism, Organization, and Management Theory. *Journal of Management Inquiry*, 25(2), 171–183. doi:10.1177/1056492615589973

Singleton, J. L., Jones, G., & Hanumantha, S. (2014). Toward ethical research practice with deaf participants. *Journal of Empirical Research on Human Research Ethics*, 9(3), 59–66. doi:10.1177/1556264614540589

Smith, L. T. (2005). On Tricky Ground: Researching the Native in the Age of Uncertainty. In N. K. Denzin & Y. S. Lincoln (Eds.), *The SAGE Handbook of Qualitative Research* (3rd ed., pp. 85–108). Thousand Oaks, CA: SAGE Publications.

Trivedi, H. (1999). The postcolonial or the transcolonial? Location and language. *Interventions: The International Journal of Postcolonial Studies*, 1(2), 269–272.

Tyson, L. (1999). *Critical Theory Today: A User-Friendly Guide*. New York: Garland.

Vambe, M. T., & Rwafa, U. (2011). Introduction: Theorising African-language literatures in the twenty-first century. *Journal of Literary Studies*, 27(3), 1.

Vermeer, H. J. (2006). *Luhmann's 'Social Systems' Theory: Preliminary Fragments for a Theory of Translation*. Berlin: Frank & Timme GmbH.

Wallace, M., & Sheldon, N. (2015). Business Research Ethics: Participant Observer Perspectives. *Journal of Business Ethics*, 128(2), 267–277. doi:10.1007/s10551-014-2102-2

Wallerstein, I. (1997). Social Science and the Quest for a Just Society. *American Journal of Sociology*, 102(5), 1241.

Whitehead, K. A. (2012). Racial categories as resources and constraints in everyday interactions: Implications for racialism and non-racialism in post-apartheid South Africa. *Ethnic & Racial Studies*, 35(7), 1248–1265. doi:10.1080/01419870.2011.591407

Widding, G. (2012). Keep a-knocking (but you can't come in): The issue of passing by the gatekeeper and gaining linguistic access to qualitative research fields. *Education Inquiry (Umea University, Education Inquiry)*, 3(3), 421–435.

William, I. (2009). Post-Colonialism, Memory and the Remaking of African Identity. *Politikon*, 36(3), 423–443, doi:10.1080/02589341003600221

4

IMPLICATIONS OF ONTOLOGY AND EPISTEMOLOGY

A researcher who investigates gender, race, identity, indigeneity, and diversity (GRIID) functions across multiple disciplines unfolds some aspects of psychological, sociological, sociopolitical, and economic conditions, creating knowledge based on assumed or perceived reality—the ontology. Therefore, the GRIID researcher, regardless of qualitative or quantitative approaches in the research method, must explain the nature of being and temporality, the ontology as a prelude to the episteme; it is important to explain the ontological and the epistemological foundation of each research to situate the study and contextualize it appropriately.

Ontology is the philosophical nature of what is, the nature of reality and categories of existence. However, the reality, being, or *Dasein* that form the *conceptual* basis of a researcher's worldview in examining GRIID topics can be illusive. As Plato (2017) recalled the conversation of his brother Glaucon and Socrates about the nature of reality as presented to us:

> the power and capacity of learning exists in the soul already; and that just as the eye was unable to turn from darkness to light without the whole body, so too the instrument of knowledge can only by the movement of the whole soul be turned from the world of becoming into that of being, and learn by degrees to endure the sight of being.
>
> *(pp. 15–16)*

A researcher's ontological position, the conceptual frame, can only be verified through its *epistemology* which explains the validity and scope of the reality and its theoretical frame as investigated. By now, perhaps the reader of this book is familiar with the essential research process such as Creswell (2014) and Patton (2002, 2015), who have addressed the basics of ontology and epistemology in general research. However, there is a tautological confusion about ontology, epistemology, quantitative vs. qualitative, and so on (Mkansi & Acheampong, 2012). Doctoral students across GRIID disciplines are familiarized into their respective programs by being trained to look for hard evidence as fashioned by the positivists, particularly in professional doctorates (Cole et al., 2011), yet the philosophical underpinning of ontological positions and epistemological perspectives is not void of metaphysical assumptions that the students must become familiar with (Chatterjee, 2013). Creating general theories to apply in a field requires realistic assessment of multi-ontological and epistemological approaches rather than thinking positivism can accomplish the task (Storberg-Walker, 2006). Some GRIID research areas such as gender, disability, ethnicity, and racialization require appropriate ontological and epistemological footing, connecting the researcher to the experience of the researched to correctly formulate a general theory or test a theory in the right light (Fawcett & Hearn, 2004).

In this chapter, first we will address how philosophical discussions have arrived at what we know about ontology and epistemology, because this is an area that is often addressed and contextualized by doctoral students inadequately. Second, following each discussion, we will review how the conceptual, the ontology, and the theoretical, the epistemology, frames influence the problem formulation, the investigation, and the outcomes in GRIID studies. We will address the implication of ontological positioning and epistemological approaches in Chapter 6, explaining how each should be delineated in various parts of writing a research proposal. Many of the ontologies and epistemologies have been defined and described in detail in other literature. Therefore, we will not attempt to redefine them here. We will discuss some of the most pertinent issues relating to GRIID research in this chapter and examine their impact.

Ontology

The nature of reality on which GRIID researchers base their investigation was first articulated by Plato (2017) in Socrates' description of the allegory of the cave, relying on senses and reasoning in determining existence. GRIID research involves humans and humanity; therefore, there is no escaping some degree of darkness in objectivity by which a researcher claims at arriving at the results. Like Plato's analogy, a GRIID researcher is feeling, touching, and describing a peculiarity of the presented condition based on the researcher's *a priori* knowledge. Thus, the *thing* which is before the researcher may not appear in front of another, making confirmability or validity difficult. Hence, providing a clear description of the how, why, and what it is that one researches is imperative.

Centuries after Plato, Kant added new complexities into the meaning of ontology by connecting metaphysics and empiricism while relying on *ens realissimum*, an unobtainable metaphysical notion of reality and noumenal view of reality, *a thing which is as opposed to what senses may perceive it* (Truwant, 2014). Kant argued that it is the pure reason that allows for scientific inquiry by disengaging the researcher from self-interest to objectively examine what is presented as an ethical imperative (Truwant, 2014). Essentially, Kant argued that it is the ethical concerns of researchers that when embodied with inner moral values would prevent them from skewing reality based on the perception and allow reality to present itself as it is. Yet Kant's (1994) argument rests on external constraints and internal free-constraints depending on one's will that control values, which present an obstacle to objectivity. Therefore, if a researcher positions an investigation ontologically based on Kant's moral values, the research objectivity can be a suspect. For example, a Northern Irish researcher investigating the role of the British in Northern Ireland's current sociological situation requires rationale as to how he or she reconciles the external constraints and internal constraints of free will in objectively explaining the study's ontology. Hegel countered Kant's innercism of morality and repositioned the discussions of ontology.

Hegel (2000) postulated that human understanding requires relation to the world rather than relying on innercism of moral values. Hegel (2000) saw the unity of immaterial mind and material body (idealism and existential world) through dialectical processes. Both Kant's and Hegel's arguments had a direct impact on how we create, expand, and consume knowledge. Their discussions of idealism vs. existentialism, mind vs. matter, provided the situatedness, the ontology of the researchers' framework in creating the episteme. However, Hegel, unlike Kant, rather than relying on innercism of moral values, or *virtues*, objectified reality through the dialectical processes of opposing forces of idealism and materialism, giving credence to what it is, or the ontology. Heidegger (1993) expanded on Hegel's arguments, explaining the human peculiarities of being and presence, using the German word *Dasein*.

Heidegger (1993), in the context of human peculiarities, explained that being and time are inextricably interwoven and, while universal, *being* is undefinable yet is self-evident by reason as a genus. Heidegger (1993) viewed ontological position as Dasein, which explains *thatness, whatness, validity*, and *existence* (p. 47). Heidegger, ontologically differentiated natural from the human sciences by explaining that the former requires coherence with itself while the latter requires aesthesis and noesis within the temporal context. Therefore, in GRIID research, the investigator must explain how perception and awareness within the temporal frame positions the study in creating knowledge. As you recall, we briefly explained the notion of social identity theory (SIT) in Chapter 1. In light of the preceding discussions of ontology, one must be aware that taking certain consequences in applying theoretical frame or testing of a theory for advancing a particular episteme. For example, when adopting SIT as the theoretical frame to explain the phenomenon under consideration, the researcher must be aware of its underpinning assumptions and its possible contradiction with Heidegger's view if the research is pursuing a phenomenological approach. Many views have provided a plethora of ontologies in positioning current research.

The unfolding of perspectives after Kant brought a variation and dissection of the ontological views, each with its own challenges. We will discuss some of the more prominent ones here briefly and we encourage the reader to expand their examination of each position in a cascading manner, starting here as the first step, following the thread of references. Reality can be framed from multiple perspectives or selection of a lens to arrive at new knowledge. From the grand ontological schemes, reality has been subject to vacillation of metaphysical underpinnings from monism, dualism, and pluralism, between mind and matter; at times the two sides became one through the dialectics and at other times each side was independent of other (Eucken & Phelps, 1880). Some philosophers have attempted to etymologically argue that mind is not the same as cognition, although cognition may be a part of it; hence, mind in itself presents pluralism ontologically (Van Gelder, 1998). More recent developments in neuroscience, building on Jungian theory, have supported the notion that mind encompasses cognition, connecting unconscious thoughts to the articulated conscious actions, unifying the mind and matter and supporting ontological monism (Bob, 2013; Ekstrom, 2004; Giannoni & Corradi, 2006; Tresan, 1996). Even within ontological monism, there exists numerous philosophical positions as to how reality can be viewed.

Among various philosophical ontologies are relativism, realism, critical realism, critical relativism, critical theory, poststructuralism, postmodernism, postindustrialism, social constructivism, feminism, intersectionalism, neo- and postcolonialism, decolonization, and deconstructivism. While we will briefly address some of these ontologies, we will provide an expanded discussion of postcolonialism, decolonization, and feminism due to their misapplication to GRIID research.

First, we will provide examples of some of the ontologies that are simpler to explain in the context of GRIID research to describe how each will influence the analysis part of the research and outcome. Relativism argues that none of the GRIID inquiries lend themselves to transcendental universal realism because the researcher attempts to understand particular human interactions that can unfold meaning based on ethnomethodology and intentionality; hence, the best a researcher can hope for is relativism (Gunnell, 2016). Realism is built upon philosophical transcendence, making its application to empirical investigations such as those conducted within GRIID scientifically impossible (Merrill, 2010). Postmodernism is a sensible way, regardless of the nature of the research, to connect and explain the research outcome to the social and ethical power of the participants, the researcher, and the social actors impacting the outcome (Richardson, 1991). Therefore, postmodernism as an ontological positioning allows for alternative research outcomes requiring the GRIID researcher to provide detailed explanation of how the outcome will hold valid across multiple projects. Postindustrialism provides a temporal setting where the explanation of economic changes and power shifts impact the study (Richmond, 1984), requiring the GRIID researcher to delineate how factors associated with it influence the research outcome and why. We also encourage the reader to review the literature such as Huff (2009), Creswell (2014), and Patton (2015) to examine how critical realism, critical relativism, critical theory, poststructuralism, social constructivism, intersectionalism, and deconstructivism may impact the analysis section of their research. Next, we will address how feminism and postcolonialism impact GRIID research because of lack of inattention in what they mean and how they can distort a research outcome if improperly used. Due to complexities and linkage of the two conceptual frames by colleagues, we will discuss postcolonialism and feminism separately and then we will examine how the postcolonial frame has impacted feminism.

To explain postcolonialism, one must first describe what colonialism is and how its creation led to what came afterwards. Colonization is the subjugation of one by another creating a master–slave relationship, where the history is rewritten by the master and the slave is marginalized without any voice; the master writes the rules, the slave must follow; the master portrays the existential consciousness, the slave becomes imprisoned by its unconscious memory of what was without the masters (Bell, 2009). Colonialism began with the West thinking of itself as the civilized and any other as uncivilized, only to revise its appearance as postcolonialism masquerading its position (Seth, Gandhi, & Dutton, 1998). Said (2004) asserted that colonialism transcends temporality, moving the discussion of colonialism from the literature and ethnological studies to the mainstream ontological examination of the topic.

Postcolonialism emerged as an intellectual movement through which time and dialogical process grew to encompass multiple disciplines from psychology to sociology, economics, politics, and other fields of humanities (Bhambra, 2014; Bowman, 2010; Chow, 1998; Patke, 2006). Postcolonialism is not about third world countries or the nature of the relationship between the North and the South; it is about the complex nature of the colonized and colonizers across boundaries, within socioeconomic, psycho-sociological, and political spheres, positioning the knowledge production in terms of relationships and power (Docker, 1995; Dutton, Gandhi, & Seth, 1999a; Ribeiro, 2011). Postcolonialism continues the Western ideals of the knowledge production of colonialism, corrupting the nature of objectivity in investigating reality rather than allowing multiple perspectives (Dutton, Gandhi, & Seth, 1999b). Gandhi (2007b) viewed the portrayal of postcolonialism as historical amnesia of colonialism which was described as "anticolonial antipositivism, antihistoricism and antimaterialism." Postcolonialism is "essentialisms, totalities, and fixities," where its epistemology addresses the ontology of the colonized and the colonizer from all intellectual and empirical aspects (Gandhi, 2007c). Some such as Harootunian (1999) have asserted that postcolonialism is about neither temporality nor entitlement by the colonized, but rather ontological positioning of the oppressed in theorizing and creating knowledge. Rooted and rising out of literature, postcoloniality does not allow reconciliation between the colonizer and the colonized; it is a continuation of colonialism attempting to mask itself as the dawn of new era where colonization has ended (Huddart, 2014; Johnson, 2011). As Tinsley (2015) argued, postcolonialism is a continuation of colonialism reflected in the way the colonized uses language etymologically in creating knowledge. Where the colonized is not able to recall his native language in describing the reality, before the colonizers arrived, then the colonizers are prevailing in how and why knowledge is produced. Therefore, a GRIID researcher must be mindful of the dangers of a postcolonial ontological worldview.

Feminist theory, rooted in the 1980s development of reconstruction of knowledge based on gender and body (Schaefer, 2014) outlines an "emancipatory value" proposition in knowledge production from a woman's perspective (Assiter, 2000). Feminism offers an ontological position for investigations and analysis in terms of a male–female power relationship, while its second wave assumed normative patriarchal domination and oppression, and its third wave has been characterized by a set of social and cultural ideas of what a girl or women should be (Schippers & Sapp, 2011). Within the neoliberal framework, feminist theory, from a sociopolitical perspective, offers a unique opportunity to produce knowledge based on procedural and distributive justice, addressing the equity and equality between men and women (Smith, 2008). Recent developments have offered some objections and limitations of the feminist worldview.

Articulated by some recent critics, feminism in its current worldview seeks to correct Habermasian communicative action by replacing "discourse of the ethics of care instead of a Habermasian ethics of justice" and supplementing it with "expressive, political narrative as a supplement to rational expressions" (Pajnik, 2006, pp. 401–402). Politically, feminism has been criticized for its narrow view of gender in terms of man and women in knowledge production and has been born out of the global North (Kantola & Lombardo, 2017; Roberts & Connell, 2016). Feminism as a worldview also presents other limitations.

Feminism, rooted in seeking justice for women and establishing equitable distributive justice for men and women by reconstructing procedural justice, has limitations in intersectional approaches to addressing many research problems. For example, addressing woman identity based on intersectionality of gender, race, sexual orientation, and disability cannot provide a democratic voice in its approach (Emejulu, 2011). Another challenge in the feminist approach to GRIID research is its ability to overcome its entanglement with postcolonialism and articulate its position more clearly vis-à-vis non-Western women (Gandhi, 2007a).

Epistemology

As Hancock (2015) reminded us, "Science is demonstration of what things are and how they exist in light of their causes" (p. 234). However, modern science represents episteme as description and control rather than reasoning (Hancock, 2015), which can challenge the validity of any quantitative studies. Knowledge development is only possible when the picture and perception are united through logical elements in the absence of universal laws (Hegel, 2000). However, the challenge of empiricism is its inability to logically avoid philosophizing corruptive and perverted arguments (Hegel, 2000, p. 69). Indeed, our theoretical underpinning provides justification for how we arrive at new knowledge. Among the epistemological approaches used in researching

GRIID are positivism, empiricism, interpretivism, critical race theory, integrative approach, humanism, ethnography, traditional, reflexive, critical, heuristic, phenomenology, case study, and narrative, just to outline some of those frequently used. We encourage our readers to examine each of these views in other sources such as Creswell (2014) and Patton (2015) and similar publications. More recently, other epistemological theories such as ecological system theory have also been applied to GRIID research.

Ecological system theory (EST) places human development, or more precisely the individual, with a nested system of environmental factors within its core where the individual begins connecting to the environment at large (Bronfenbrenner, 2009; Heberle, 1952). EST allows cognitive reflection on complex relationship with each nested environment at any point in time and each set of circumstance, providing necessary explanations where cultural connections are difficult to make (Bronfenbrenner, 2009).

Ontological and epistemological juxtaposition, and methodology

The ontological position of a research proposal offers a lens by which the researcher examines a problem. An epistemological approach provides the mechanics of knowledge production. While epistemological approaches in quantitative studies allow generalizability and demonstrating reliability, they are at odds with the ontology of meaning within GRIID qualitative studies (Wakefield, 1995). In GRIID studies, a researcher requires both an ontological and epistemological explanation of how meaning has been created or how causality can demonstrate an irrefutable connection between an outcome and the source. In quantitative studies where researchers take a positivist epistemological position to demonstrate generalizability and reliability, they fail to point out that the findings face uncertainty and the causes remain under scrutiny unless, over time, all attempts to prove the findings wrong fail (Scotland, 2012). On the other hand, in qualitative studies, the narratives of human experiences are suspect ontologically and epistemologically based on the differences of the stories told and the experiences lived (Meretoja, 2014). Morgan and Smircich (1980) argued that on the subjectivity–objectivity spectrum, the ontological and epistemological position can be changed to suit an argument, rendering the methodological process incapable of creating anything concrete. Therefore, a GRIID researcher, on the subjectivity–objectivity continuum, must provide the logical assumptions underpinning the ontology and the epistemology of the research subjects and explain their compatibility in creating reliability and validity in the study.

Summary

Exploration of the impact of ontological and epistemological perspectives on research results deserves attention in GRIID studies. Ontological positioning provides the narrative by which the researcher has been examining the topic, while epistemological positioning provides the formulation of the process by which new knowledge has been created. In inductive and abductive qualitative research, the researcher is the instrument; therefore, his or her ontological orientation is imperative in the way data has been collected and analyzed. In quantitative research, the deductive processes of the data collection tools require reliance on well-defined epistemology of theories and the ontological reasoning why those theories have been claimed to be valid before testing them.

EXERCISES

a   Examine the wording in your problem statement and focus on the specific problem. Based on the wording, how would you create the purpose statement to reflect the research ontological and epistemological position? Write your purpose statement and describe the process.

b   Where in your dissertation should you describe your ontological and epistemological perspectives? Write what you would write in those sections.

References

Assiter, A. (2000). Feminist epistemology and value. *Feminist Theory*, 1(3), 329–345. doi:10.1177/14647000022229263

Bell, A. (2009). A Conversation through History: Towards Postcolonial Coexistence. *Journal of Intercultural Studies*, 30(2), 173–191. doi:10.1080/07256860902766974

Bhambra, G. K. (2014). Postcolonial and decolonial dialogues. *Postcolonial Studies*, 17(2), 115–121. doi:10.1080/13688790.2014.966414

Bob, P. (2013). Dissociation, chaos and transcendent function. *Activitas Nervosa Superior*, 55(4), 151–156.

Bowman, P. (2010). Rey Chow, postcoloniality and interdisciplinarity. *Postcolonial Studies*, 13(3), 231–238. doi:10.1080/13688790.2010.508813

Bronfenbrenner, U. (2009). *The Ecology of Human Development: Experiments by Nature and Design*. Cambridge, MA: Harvard University Press.

Chatterjee, A. (2013). Ontology, Epistemology, and Multimethod Research in Political Science. *Philosophy of the Social Sciences*, 43(1), 73–99.

Chow, R. (1998). The postcolonial difference: Lessons in cultural legitimation. *Postcolonial Studies*, 1(2), 161–169. doi:10.1080/13688799890110

Cole, C., Chase, S., Couch, O., & Clark, M. (2011). Research Methodologies and Professional Practice: Considerations and Practicalities. *Electronic Journal of Business Research Methods*, 9(2), 141–151.

Creswell, J. W. (2014). *Research Design: Qualitative, Quantitative, and Mixed Methods Approaches* (4th ed.). Thousand Oaks, CA: SAGE Publications.

Docker, J. (1995). Rethinking postcolonialism and multiculturalism in the fin de siècle. *Cultural Studies*, 9(3), 409–426.

Dutton, M., Gandhi, L., & Seth, S. (1999a). Watch this space. *Postcolonial Studies*, 2(3), 279–281. doi:10.1080/13688799989599

Dutton, M., Gandhi, L., & Seth, S. (1999b). The toolbox of postcolonialism. *Postcolonial Studies*, 2(2), 121–124. doi:10.1080/13688799989706

Ekstrom, S. R. (2004). The mind beyond our immediate awareness: Freudian, Jungian, and cognitive models of the unconscious. *The Journal of Analytical Psychology*, 49(5), 657–682.

Emejulu, A. (2011). Re-theorizing feminist community development: towards a radical democratic citizenship. *Community Development Journal*, 46(3), 378–390.

Eucken, R., & Phelps, M. S. (1880). Monism–Dualism. In *The Fundamental Concepts of modern Philosophic Thought, Critically and Historically Considered* (pp. 113–134). New York, NY: D Appleton & Company.

Fawcett, B., & Hearn, J. (2004). Researching others: epistemology, experience, standpoints and participation. *International Journal of Social Research Methodology*, 7(3), 201–218. doi:10.1080/13645570210163989

Gandhi, L. (2007a). *Postcolonial Theory: A Critical Introduction*. New York: Columbia University Press.

Gandhi, L. (2007b). Postcolonial theory and the crisis of European man. *Postcolonial Studies*, 10(1), 93–110. doi:10.1080/13688790601153180

Gandhi, L. (2007c). About exception. *Postcolonial Studies*, 10(2), 123–126. doi:10.1080/13688790701348532

Giannoni, M., & Corradi, M. (2006). How the mind understands other minds: Cognitive psychology, attachment and reflective function. *Journal of Analytical Psychology*, 51(2), 271–284. doi:10.1111/j.0021-8774.2006.00587.x

Gunnell, J. G. (2016). Social Inquiry and the Pursuit of Reality: Cora Diamond and the Problem of Criticizing from "Outside". *Philosophy of the Social Sciences*, 46(6), 584–603.

Hancock, C. L. (2015). The One and the Many: The Ontology of Science in Aristotle and Thomas Aquinas. *Review of Metaphysics*, 69(2), 233.

Harootunian, H. D. (1999). Postcoloniality's unconscious/area studies' desire. *Postcolonial Studies*, 2(2), 127–147. doi:10.1080/13688799989715

Heberle, R. (1952). On Political Ecology. *Social Forces*, 31(1), 1–9.

Hegel, G. W. F. (2000). *Natural Law: The Scientific Ways of Treating Natural Law, Its Place in Moral Philosophy, and Its Relation to the Positive Sciences of Law* (T. M. Knox, Trans.). Philadelphia: University of Pennsylvania Press.

Heidegger, M. (1993). *Basic Writings: From Being and Time (1927) to The Task of Thinking (1964)* (Rev. and expanded ed.) (D. F. Krell, Ed.). San Francisco, CA: HarperSanFrancisco.

Huddart, D. (2014). Comparatively slow: Postcolonial meandering. *Postcolonial Studies*, 17(4), 367–381. doi:10.1080/13688790.2014.967335

Huff, A. S. (2009). *Designing Research for Publication*. Los Angeles: SAGE Publications.

Johnson, M. (2011). Reconciliation, indigeneity, and postcolonial nationhood in settler states. *Postcolonial Studies*, 14(2), 187–201. doi:10.1080/13688790.2011.563457

Kant, I. (1994). *Ethical Philosophy* (2nd ed.) (J. W. Ellington, Trans.). Indianapolis, IN: Hackett.

Kantola, J., & Lombardo, E. (2017). Feminist political analysis: Exploring strengths, hegemonies and limitations. *Feminist Theory*, 18(3), 323–341.

Meretoja, H. (2014). Narrative and Human Existence: Ontology, Epistemology, and Ethics. *New Literary History*, 45(1), 89–109. doi:10.1353/nlh.2014.0001

Merrill, G. H. (2010). Realism and reference ontologies: Considerations, reflections and problems. *Applied Ontology*, 5(3–4), 189–221. doi:10.3233/AO-2010-0080

Mkansi, M., & Acheampong, E. A. (2012). Research Philosophy Debates and Classifications: Students' Dilemma. *Electronic Journal of Business Research Methods*, 10(2), 132–140.

Morgan, G., & Smircich, L. (1980). The Case for Qualitative Research. *Academy of Management Review*, 5(4), 491–500. doi:10.5465/AMR.1980.4288947

Pajnik, M. (2006). Feminist Reflections on Habermas's Communicative Action: The Need for an Inclusive Political Theory. *European Journal of Social Theory*, 9(3), 385–404. doi:10.1177/1368431006065719

Patke, R. S. (2006). Postcolonial Cultures. *Theory, Culture & Society*, 23(2–3), 369–372.

Patton, M. Q. (2002). *Qualitative Research and Evaluation Methods* (3rd ed.). Thousand Oaks, CA: SAGE Publications.

Patton, M. Q. (2015). *Qualitative Research and Evaluation Methods: Integrating Theory and Practice* (4th ed.). Thousand Oaks, CA: SAGE Publications.

Plato. (2017). *The Allegory of the Cave (Illustrated)* (pp. 15–16). Lulu.com. Kindle Edition.

Ribeiro, G. L. (2011). Why (post)colonialism and (de)coloniality are not enough: A post-imperialist perspective. *Postcolonial Studies*, 14(3), 285–297. doi:10.1080/13688790.2011.613107

Richardson, L. (1991). Postmodern Social Theory: Representational Practices. *Sociological Theory*, 9(2), 173–179.

Richmond, A. H. (1984). Ethic nationalism and postindustrialism. *Ethnic & Racial Studies*, 7(1), 4–18.

Roberts, C., & Connell, R. (2016). Feminist theory and the global South. *Feminist Theory*, 17(2), 135–140.

Said, E. W. (2004). *Orientalism* (25th ed.). New York: Vintage Books.

Seth, S., Gandhi, L., & Dutton, M. (1998). Postcolonial studies: A beginning…. *Postcolonial Studies*, 1(1), 7–11. doi:10.1080/13688799890200

Schaefer, D. O. (2014). Embodied Disbelief: Poststructural Feminist Atheism. *Hypatia*, 29(2), 371–387. doi:10.1111/hypa.12039

Schippers, M., & Sapp, E. (2011). Reading Pulp Fiction's Fabienne: Embodied Femininity and Power in Second and Third Wave Feminist Theory. *Conference Papers–American Sociological Association*, 2146.

Scotland, J. (2012). Exploring the Philosophical Underpinnings of Research: Relating Ontology and Epistemology to the Methodology and Methods of the Scientific, Interpretive, and Critical Research Paradigms. *English Language Teaching*, 5(9), 9–16.

Smith, A. M. (2008). Neoliberalism, welfare policy, and feminist theories of social justice. *Feminist Theory*, 9(2), 131–144. doi:10.1177/1464700108090407

Storberg-Walker, J. J. (2006). From imagination to application: Making the case for the general method of theory-building research in applied disciplines. *Human Resource Development International*, 9(2), 227–259. doi:10.1080/13678860600616420

Tinsley, M. (2015). Proclaiming Independence: Language and National Identity in Sékou Touré's Guinea. *Postcolonial Studies*, 18(3), 237–256. doi:10.1080/13688790.2015.1105126

Tresan, D. I. (1996). Jungian metapsychology and neurobiological theory. *The Journal of Analytical Psychology*, 41(3), 399–436. doi:10.1111/j.1465-5922.1996.00399.x

Truwant, S. (2014). The Turn from Ontology to Ethics: Three Kantian Responses to Three Levinasian Critiques. *International Journal of Philosophical Studies*, 22(5), 696–715. doi:10.1080/09672559.2014.917692

Van Gelder, T. (1998). Monism, dualism, pluralism. *Mind & Language*, 13(1), 76–97. doi:10.1111/1468-0017.00066

Wakefield, J. C. (1995). When an irresistible epistemology meets an immovable ontology. *Social Work Research*, 19(1), 9–17.

5

RESEARCH DESIGN

In Chapter 1, we discussed gender, race, identity, indigeneity, and diversity (GRIID) research involving complex connections between individual identity that may be manifested by attitudes, behaviors, actions as verbalized by individuals, and individual identity that is manifested psychologically (consciously or unconsciously), sociologically (as identified through race, gender, family, or tribe), or both. Chapter 1 also provided operational definitions and examined the connection between identity and various elements of GRIID research. Chapter 2 explained the role of procedural and distributive justice in GRIID research and how the concepts influence the nature of a research outcome. Chapters 3 and 4 examined the role of ethics, ontology, and epistemology in research. In this chapter, we will focus on addressing the unique requirements of GRIID research methodology. The intent of this chapter is to explain the roadmap for determining the methods, designs, and approaches to GRIID research rather than explaining their mechanics; other publications have already provided sufficient in-depth explanation about the mechanics (i.e., Creswell, 2014; Patton, 2015). First, we will review the general principles which are applicable to any research. Second, we will turn our focus to discussing the particularities of GRIID methodologies requirements.

The research method is a function of the problem statement. If we assume that $y = ax + b$, where y is the method, then x is the problem statement, a is attributes of the problem and its nuances, and b is the setting within which the problem resides. Therefore, before thinking about what method should be used, the problem should be articulated clearly, providing what are the ax and b. A correctly formulated problem statement should help:

- Justify the alignment of theory with qualitative/quantitative approach, research purpose, and research questions.
- Develop a qualitative/quantitative research plan that is aligned with respect to research problem, purpose, question, and approach.

- Develop an interview/survey guide that is aligned with and uses appropriate terminology for the research purpose, question, and approach.
- Develop and implement a qualitative/quantitative research plan, including instrument development, participant selection and recruitment, pilot testing, transcribing, and analyzing data.
- Determine appropriate data collection, data management, and data analysis techniques for different qualitative/quantitative approaches.
- Justify use of qualitative/quantitative reasoning and analysis, with the intent of developing competence for the research.
- Analyze qualitative/quantitative research for social justice implications.

The roadmap can be something like that suggested by Table 3.1. The researcher should link the components correctly to assure alignment between the problem, the purpose, the research question, the nature, and its significance sections. Once the problem with its attributes and its setting is clearly identified, then one can move to formulating the purpose of the research, arriving at a method to investigate the problem. Before thinking about the method, the researcher should

1.   Conduct a comprehensive literature review to identify a gap in the literature or assess a gap in practice. The approach depends on the doctoral program requirements and the extent that the degree program is focused on clinical, experimental, or theoretical foundations. In clinical or experimental research, the previous research results should be closely examined, and the nature of experiments, the inconsistencies, and even the source of funding should be reviewed for the possible flawed results or areas where additional research is required and the context within which previous experiments should be re-examined.

Example of stating the background, indicating the gap

Exclusion of women from leadership positions and inequality in gender roles could impede women's development as leaders. Women around the world are experiencing gender bias that presents obstacles to their progress in leadership at political, social, and organizational levels (Kakabadse et al., 2015; Seierstad, Warner Søderholm, Torchia, & Huse, 2017).

---

1.   Formulate a problem statement based on the gap identified.

   a   A hook, explaining and drawing the readers' attention (must be interesting to stimulate the readers' thoughts and think about the *wow* that the research outcome will present).

b Should have a general problem (supported by the literature or, in practice-based and clinical cases, should provide the challenges of current
practices to support the claim).

c Should have a specific problem, within the general problem scope (supported by literature or, in practice-based and clinical cases, should provide
the challenges of current practices to support the claim).

d Should be concise and no more than two-thirds of one page and should
be two or three paragraphs; otherwise would lead to many ambiguities
impacting other sections of the research.

Example of using a hook to draw the reader in with social significance addressing an issue as within the identity continuum (see Figure 5.1)

Women's exclusion from leadership positions could affect more than governance practices, hindering gender diversity and equity on corporate boards.
In 2012, survey results from corporate boards of directors of participating
public and private companies in 59 countries indicated that 87% of women
reported experiencing gender-related barriers, and 56% of men disagreed with
the women's perception (Groysberg & Bell, 2013). Gender bias is an unconscious prejudice embedded in an individual's background, culture, and personal experiences with women (Cook & Glass, 2014, pp. 6–7).

The problem statement section can proceed with the general and specific problem in
theoretical studies based on the literature as illustrated in the example below or clinical
information or work-based gaps in intervention as the degree program may require:

Example

The general problem of interest in this study was that organizations could lose
the values that women bring to the workplace in leadership positions because of
gender bias. By exploring how women on corporate boards cope with gender
bias, it is possible to address a major gap in the current research literature. The
specific problem was that gender bias could influence women's roles on a corporate board, which can affect their appointment, can be disruptive to board
dynamics, and can create a need to develop coping strategies to deal with gender
bias as women execute their roles on a corporate board (pp. 7–8).

---

1. Based on the nature of the specific problem, a research question should be
stated, determining the theoretical framing of the inquiry, the method (i.e.,
heuristic, ethnography, or experimental). Several hypotheses should be generated to allow for quantitative or experimental approaches.

Example
  How does a woman describe her experiences dealing with gender bias; how can gender bias influence her role on a corporate board; how can gender bias affect her appointment that could be disruptive to board dynamics; and how can gender bias create a need to develop coping strategies to deal with gender bias as she executes her role on a corporate board? (p. 9)

1. The conceptual framework should explain the lens by which the researcher is examining the topic and the theories that help address the problem.

   a Conceptual frame: postmodernist, constructivist, deconstructionist, feminist, etc. (some doctoral programs use the *conceptual frame* as explanation of underlying theories explaining the approach to examination of the problem in qualitative or quantitative methods).
   b Theoretical frame: for example, leadership theories if the problem is addressing leadership, intersectionality if a number of concepts will merge into one in addressing social issues, etc. (some doctoral programs use the *theoretical frame* as explanation of underlying theories explaining the approach to examination of the problem in qualitative or quantitative methods).
   c In quantitative research, often the theoretical and conceptual framework is explained in the literature review chapter and used when explaining the data in the discussions section.

The domain of inquiry must be within the PhD program or the researcher's field as required by the program or publication. For example, if it is a dissertation within

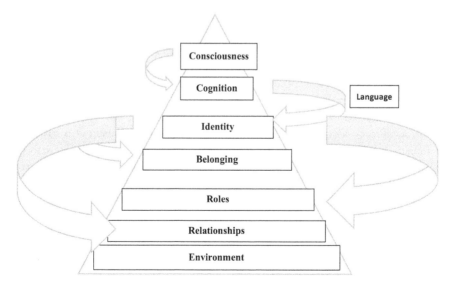

FIGURE 5.1 Identity Continuum

organizational leadership, the problem should be a sub-field of the program and cannot be something different. Therefore, when formulating the problem statement, the wording should reflect the domain and the degree program and the focus of the study within that sub-field. The wording should provide continuity in the purpose, nature, research questions, theoretical and conceptual frame, and the literature review.

When conducting research, the alignment between the problem statement, the purpose, the research question, the nature of the study, and the method should be the researcher's focus. The alignment requires precise wording in different components of the prospectus (the preliminary draft synopsis of the proposal) and later how those words are used in various chapters of the proposal and the dissertation. While in qualitative studies the problem statement wording dictates the type of qualitative research method, in quantitative studies the wording should reflect relations or correlations between variables, allowing for stating null and alternative hypotheses. Mixed methods is normally the result of the nature of the stated problem and how both meaning and correlations are intertwined in the research process. Too often the wording in the problem statement leads to misalignment with the selected method. Therefore, careful crafting of a problem statement can alleviate the alignment issues, resulting in a well-designed research proposal. What, then, drives the writing of a problem? How does a researcher start in stating a problem? What would be the nature of the problem statement? This chapter will answer these questions in addition to determining the method for GRIID research and how to align various components of the research proposal.

Before stating the problem, the researcher, based on the nature of degree program and profession, must determine the type of issues that require investigation. The GRIID researcher must determine if the problem is related to an application or a general inquiry based on the literature. Applied research or practice-based degree programs may require understanding/testing of relationships between variables such as how would one respond to a stimulus, assessing intervention to correct a behavior, or similar types of problems. Alternatively, the literature review may reveal a gap in knowledge about gender, race, identity, indigeneity, and diversity. In the former instance, the problem statement should be stated based on the applied work (practice) requiring further clarification and understanding to improve application or intervention. In the latter, the review of the literature reveals a gap in knowledge, which becomes the problem. Therefore, as a starting point, applied or literature-based are two distinct ways of arriving at a problem statement, yet both require articulating something significant, a type of clue as to why the research is required, the general nature of the problem and a specific area of the problem that will be examined. Generally, we have three broad methods in conducting research: (1) qualitative, (2) quantitative, and (3) mixed methods.

In GRIID research where the identity and diversity are constructed differently (based on the conceptual, or the author's lens, and the theoretical, or the author's use of theories to explain the problem), the nature of diversity is composed differently, leading the research into different directions (Harrison & Klein, 2007). Therefore, when explaining the background, the attributes of identity and diversity should be fully and clearly explained.

Theoretical and conceptual frames

Generally, there are two ways to arrive at knowledge based on scientific theory building: (a) generalization based on empirical evidence arriving at a set of laws or (b) axiomatic theory based on definitions, axioms, and propositions (Reynolds, 1986). When conducting GRIID research, the researcher should be mindful of whether there is sufficiently developed context and practical understanding of the topic in the field and by the research subjects. If the answer to the question is no, then a researcher should proceed in using qualitative research, using the empirical evidence from the investigation to develop a set of generalized laws. If the answer is yes to the question, then a researcher can use the already established definitions, axioms, and propositions to arrive at axiomatic theory. Theory building has many implications for a GRIID researcher; it allows creating meaning and making sense of the research, provides an appropriate spatiotemporal epitome approach to think through the research process in arriving at a sensible form of new knowledge, allows theory building or testing the theories, forces researchers to clearly define the theoretical underpinning of the investigation and their conceptual frame (worldview), and facilitates connecting the method to the theoretical and conceptual frames.

Creating meaning

Perhaps, through the development of scientific inquiries, we have missed an etymological opportunity to re-examine the context of meaning when theorizing or testing a theory. Regardless of the scientific discipline, we normally use the word *discover* to denote finding something implying that the thing was lost. This incorrect etymological reference has led to limiting of our intellectual capacity in understanding social issues, particularly in GRIID research. Each time we examine a phenomenon, we learn new things about it and improve our understanding of it, whereas the phenomenon exists independent of our thoughts and remains the same. Applying the allegory of the cave, "this entire allegory, I said, you may now append, dear Glaucon, to the previous argument; the prison-house is the world of sight, the light of the fire is the sun" (Plato, 2017, p. 11). Therefore, in GRIID research across disciplines to examine a range of issues (from cognitive, behavioral, social, sociological, to political and economic) and explicate meaning, operational definitions must be clarified, the nature of its construct for theorizing should be explained, and in quantitative studies its dimensions must be detailed and the unstandardized coefficients substantively analyzed (Hughes, Price, & Marrs, 1986).

In our effort to create meaning, the social construct, the researcher's reorientation (the situatedness), and the methodological approach help us to *understand, realize,* and *make sense,* rather than *discover* the phenomenon under consideration within its proper context. When examining problems such as identity, indigeneity, and culture, the created meaning must reflect a holistic approach, providing a macro, micro, or meso context of social relationships to enable us to address social justice, make a positive impact, and provide a pathway for policy making or serving the social needs (Crow, 2000). When a researcher attempts to create meaning by examining a social or cultural problem related to identity, the researcher's reorientation is required to adjust to the given realities of the setting rather than operating within his or her own social and cultural orientation, properly dealing with the social justice issues (Razack, 2005). In qualitative studies, often some form of phenomenological method can help create meaning by converging the expected (noema) and the mode of experiencing (noesis; Sanders, 1982). In applied research, where one might rely on experimental or quasi-experimental design to examine the effects of interventions, meaningful results depend on absence of process and data contamination (Bickman, Rog, & Hedrick, 2003). In applied research, adequate shared meaning by the researcher and the subject should exist to make sure the meaning and the context of communication between the researchers and the research participants does not skew the results. For example, if an applied researcher administers a survey to determine correlation between identity and national culture in Umukabia, a village in Ohuhu community of Umuahia North local government area, Abia State, Nigeria, adequate safeguards must exist in establishing etymologically shared meaning of the questions about every aspect of the terms *identity* and *national culture*, and the wording used to determine the correlation.

Fluidity vs. spatiotemporal epitome approach

GRIID research occupies a fluid spatial and temporal space, challenging the researcher's ethics, the methodological rigor and its scientific schema, and the conceptual frame in examining the problem. The GRIID spatial and temporal spaces sometimes change our references to experiences and the way we examine them (Fielding, 2014)—for example, the emphasis on feminism and the counter-culture conceptual frame, the emergence of theoretical perspectives such as postmodernism in the 1960s in the United States as a response to social changes, or emphasizing decolonization as a conceptual frame and poststructuralism as the theoretical underpinning in examining African research after the end of Apartheid. In some GRIID disciplines such as organizational studies, due to changes in the organizational boundaries and profiles and methodological inventiveness, the nature of the research approach remains fluid (Buchanan & Bryman, 2007). For example, as the power relationship within and without organizational boundaries changes and methodological rigidity gives way to expanded intellectual curiosity, the research protocols become more fluid.

There may be more challenges than those we will address in this section. However, we intend to highlight a few prominent challenges to the existing spatiotemporal epitome approach by suggesting how fluidity in methodological protocols and the researcher's frame can help maintain rigor and soundness through re-examination of the processes and adjusting to diverse existential realities.

One of the challenges that research will encounter is the method by which it has acquired an internal review board's (IRB) permission and reconciled its requirements with the nature of relationship with the participants for acquisition of accurate data. For example, when a researcher with a feminist, decolonizing conceptual frame attempts to collect data about experiences of a female from a country that has been subject to colonization and has a different type of social relationship in her own country, and the participant–researcher relationship is constantly renegotiated, the adherence to IRB requirements becomes subject to interpretation (Bhattacharya, 2007). Among other challenges are the nature of quality in selected methods (Bryman, 2006), the non-linearality and relational nature of research in indigenous studies (Lavallée, 2009), addressing social justice within indigenous research requiring participatory action while remaining neutral for objectivity (Nicholls, 2009), or the juxtaposition of the researcher's social position vis-à-vis the individuals or groups under study (Berger, 2015).

Theories

In social sciences, theories serve as the environment within which the research is conducted, providing instrumentality for conducting the research and offering alternative perspectives for analyzing the data (Bickman & Rog, 1998). In qualitative research, theories create a "system of concepts, assumptions, expectations, and beliefs" (Maxwell, 1996, p. 25). Therefore, in qualitative research theories allow the researcher to contextualize the epistemological underpinning for examining the research question and the ontological perspective examining it. Quantitative theory building requires its units to be identified, the laws of interaction applicable to the units of the theory established, its boundaries determined, and its specification of the system and its effects stated, providing a theoretical frame, proceeding to proposition specification, identification of empirical indicators for the key terms within it, hypothesis construction, and purposeful research development for testing it (Lynham, 2002). Sometimes, to bridge the gap, in fields such as counseling, theories must first be developed and then tested, creating a bridge between practice-based research based on induction and testing the theory for the results deductively (Southern & Devlin, 2010). Theory development or testing theories in GRIID research requires examination of a deeper layer of challenges.

GRIID research requires examination of relationship between consciousness, cognition, identity, belonging, roles, relationships, and environment, and the influence of meditating and moderating factors. In GRIID research, it is essential to address the extent to which elements influence each other in providing a clear picture of the phenomenon under study, contextualizing the research objective, and in testing theories explaining the intervening and intermediary factors. The examination of these factors is important because the researcher and the research subject fall within this continuum; therefore, situating and contextualizing their position are imperatives to the objectivity of findings. As shown in Figure 5.1, there is an identity relationship continuum from consciousness to environment.

Identity conveys the interplay of consciousness manifestation and self-conceptualization vis-à-vis the external world. Identity is self-conceptualization, internally constructed, incorporating roles, attributes, relationship in social organizations, and belonging by geographical location and social environment (Devine-Wright & Clayton, 2010). Internally, identity is rooted in the generalized abstract concepts perceived in one's consciousness and moved to controlled actionable thoughts through cognitive process (Gentsch et al., 2016), and represents cognitive processes perceiving the world and translating the perception into behavior (de Vries, 2004). Externally, identity is inextricably a sense of belonging based on social diversity, the changing nature of mediating factors such as technology, roles, institutions, traditions (Hall, 2013), and bicultural situatedness (Chiao et al., 2010). Other mediating and moderating factors influencing the *identity continuum* are language, experience, and emotions.

Using language to communicate complex ideas in pictorial and textual compositionality, roles, and relationships, is a distinct human attribute which has temporal situatedness (Rabagliati, Doumas, & Bemis, 2017). While language internally provides a verbal tool and visual cues interpreting consciousness and abstract perceptions through cognition, externally it is a medium for communicating the environmental factors in realizing one's identity (Strickland, 2017). Experience provides the bases for future decision making and behavior, differentiating individuals (Weiss-Cohen et al., 2018). Emotions, manifested by various cues such as facial expression, physical posturing, and voice tone embedded in the *identity continuum* rationalize individual attitudes and behavior generated by cognitive processes (Gross, 2002). Language, experience, and emotions moderate the researcher's objectivity, posing a limitation, and they may lead to subjectivity of the research participants or the way they become engaged or respond to the research process.

Frames

As a GRIID researcher, one can rely on a range of frames ontologically and epistemologically to conduct studies. Ontology—derived from the Greek word that means *to be*—is a system of organizing and helping to classify the researcher's worldview in creating knowledge (Pieterse & Kourie, 2014). The range can include traditional to postpositivist and anything in between such as feminist, Marxist, or constructionist. Regardless of the worldview, one must recognize that all knowledge is conjectural (Creswell, 2014). For example, within the positivist worldview, complexity theory in applied sciences is a probability model that allows examining different outcomes from a given set of circumstances. However, the model itself is based on agreement by those who use it without any universal truth and until the model is proven incorrect when a new situation arises in physics or astrophysics. Epistemology is "the philosophical discipline that studies the evaluative dimensions of cognition, their metaphysical bases, and the language we use to ascribe cognitive states" (Turri, 2014, p. xi). Epistemology explains the selected process for creating knowledge which includes empirical, propositional, and collective forms. While an ontological perspective situates the research, epistemology explains its process within the ontological position; for example, a proposed study can examine Canadian aboriginal psychological health with a constructionist worldview employing an empirical approach such as ethnography.

In GRIID research, the identity continuum positioning of the problem state-ment must be considered before adopting an ontological perspective and deciding on an epistemological choice. For example, if one is to study the plight of Rohingya refugees, what aspect of their dilemma is being examined based on the problem statement, and what does the research outcome hope to learn? In this example, one must review the options for framing the researcher's worldview and the process in creating the outcome. Based on the available options, the researcher must reason which worldview will most effectively situate the problem and what process will yield the most accurate outcome. Finally, GRIID researchers must be mindful of social justice implication in their research.

In Chapter 1 we examined the nature and impact of social justice in undertaking GRIID research. Deontologically, the researcher, the participants, or others can and may have a moral position in viewing the procedural and distributive justice when reflecting on any personal or social issues (O'Reilly, Aquino, & Skarlicki, 2016). Therefore, when embarking on GRIID research, the moral identity of the researcher, the research participants, and the third party must a part of the framing to effectively answer the research questions in examining the implications of the nature of perceived social justice by anyone who is directly or indirectly involved in the research process to fully grasp its impact on the research outcome.

Connecting the method to the research frame

A frame is a view of the reality within the outlines of a window, given a certain mental model for observation; it is a way of organizing representations of auditory, visual, textual interactions, relationships, and artifacts such as communication medium, and manifestation of perceptual space and temporality (Hurdley & Dicks, 2011). Given the extended multidisciplinary GRIID domains, the frames vary with regard to the nature of justice, power, identity, diversity, social, political, and eco-nomic intermediaries, and the methods are fragmented based on the peculiarities of the frames (Buchanan & Bryman, 2007). A method is the process by which the results of observation can be examined, analyzed, and interpreted; it enables the GRIID researcher to test the assumptions for the purpose of social enquiry, given the applicable emic or etic intermediaries (Hurdley & Dicks, 2011).

Emic or etic situatedness of a study will fundamentally change the frame, the window through which we examine the subject, and the ontological positioning of the research. While adopting emic approaches provides a frame to examine GRIID inquiries from an autochthonous view, etic approaches offer a universal perspective, homogenizing differences, ignoring temporality, spatiality, and etymology (Eck-ensberger, 2015). Emic approaches provide peculiarities of GRIID domains which can bring to the surface the minutest differences; when supplemented with etic views, the study can offer the imperatives such as the idea of right and wrong (Buckley et al., 2014). To determine an appropriate frame for a GRIID study, the researcher must first determine the context arising from the problem statement as we previously explained. Second, the researcher must move from the wording of the problem statement to framing the nature of examination. Third, based on the emic or etic nature of the study, or their combination, an appropriate method can be selected.

Method is dictated by the problem

Wording in the problem statement provides clues about the required method, which should be reflected in the purpose statement. Neutral wording such as *understanding, capturing, examining* a phenomenon denotes qualitative, whereas relational phrases describe quantitative or experimental methods. GRIID research, part of the social science research space, is rooted in its philosophical dimension, ontology and epistemology, where the outcome normally indicates some sort of existential reality independent of the researcher and the subject, allowing selection of methodology for investigating a problem based on the researcher's axiom (Wahyuni, 2012).

In GRIID research, analysis depends on attitudinal justice. In Chapter 2, we addressed why it is important in GRIID research to focus on distributive justice to make sure the research considers (a) the impact of social good distribution on the analysis and result of a research, (b) the worth of achieving justice, and (c) the consequences of just and unjust actions. Here, we must discuss how attitudinal justice influences the research outcome. Liebig, Sauer, and Friedhoff (2015) outlined five problems of attitudinal justice related to acquiring and analyzing data. The problems are: (1) lack of contextualization, particularly in survey-based study, creating bias, (2) lack of sufficient transparency about the factors that would influence the study, (3) lack of attention to the sociocultural structure of the study and how various groups may be impacted as a result of the study, (4) focusing on the social desirability of the study, resulting in erroneous conclusions, and (5) the way causal relationships are measured.

Method, although dependent on the ontology and epistemology, offers only three choices in conducting any enquiries—abductive, inductive, and deductive. Abductive reasoning is not deductive, yet constrained by it, based on its affirmative consequences used for solving puzzling phenomena (Lycke, 2012). Abductive reasoning is based on a novel observation that provides inferences to the best explanations, a way to use a different method interpreting data, logically and etymologically. Generally, abductive reasoning requires meta logical abstraction where theoretical logic can explain the episteme of the facts (Soler-Toscano, Fernández-Duque, & Nepomuceno-Fernández, 2012). Essentially, abduction approximates truth but does not arrive at it (Cevolani, 2013), a backward-looking deductive reasoning with specified conditions explaining the logic of inferences (Lycke, 2012). The theoretical syllogism required for abductive reasoning is complex and may not prove fruitful where the researcher is conducting his or her first scientific enquiry within the GRIID domains for a dissertation. Perhaps to mitigate risks associated with the research process, an investigator undertaking a dissertation would be advised to adopt inductive, deductive reasoning, or a combination of the two, in creating knowledge.

Qualitative challenges and appropriateness

Qualitative research can be used for theoretical and clinical research. Although there are some reservations by clinical researchers, the process and rigor apply equally (Tai & Ajjawi, 2016). The serious challenges that a GRIID researcher may face across disciplines are the avoidance of (a) manipulation of the setting or the problem of what is to be investigated and (b) imposing *a priori* on the outcome (Lincoln & Guba, 1985), which we will explain. Qualitative research may have a fixed design with a standard arrangement or may result from a logical progression of the tasks resulting from the generation of data (Maxwell, 1998). Qualitative research can be inductive, deductive, or abductive.

Qualitative research can rely on transitive inferences in analyzing the data. For example, if A > B and B > C, then A > C which is preceded by the researcher's heuristic assessment of the premise, integrating the property of the relations as outlined in the problem statement (Ameel, Verschueren, & Schaeken, 2007). As Koro-Ljungberg (2010, p. 603) suggested in qualitative studies, validity can refer to *authenticity, credibility, confirmability, internal coherence, transferability, reliability,* and *significance.* Validity requires singularity of focus and absence of aporia within social reality, avoiding transcendental ontology, linking the subject to the theory (Koro-Ljungberg, 2010).

When conducting community-based research such as investigating indigenous problems, the Delphi method can provide a unique way of seeking out knowledge that is rooted in the indigenous population and can provide a practical beginning for additional research (Brady, 2015). The Delphi method provides a practical way of obtaining maximum variation of expertise from within an indigenous population, allowing continual theory building based on participants' consensus (Brady, 2015). The Delphi method facilitates the anonymous statement of experts (Bloor et al., 2015) from the indigenous groups who by consensus can help inform and transfer knowledge from the indigenous perspective to those from outside the group.

When the research is focused on clinical examination of individuals, integrating personal philosophy with narrative psychology provides a personalist, allowing a qualitative research, which helps unfold the experiences or assessment of the nature of required intervention (Paternostro & Marcotte, 2011). The social network method allows the researcher to examine the primacy of social connections and structural patterns and capture the complexity and uniqueness of the individual factors involved (Kilduff, Tsai, & Hanke, 2006).

Quantitative reasoning and implications

As previously mentioned, the quantitative method comprises of two stages—development and testing (Lynham, 2002). Generally both stages are intertwined; as the theory is tested, refinements are made developing and modifying the theory. The quantitative method allows for detection of emerging patterns and identifying anomalies based on intervening or moderating factors (Haig, 2008); it focuses on testing a theory (Ong, 2012). The quantitative method uses deductive reasoning to test a theory; hence, it possesses certain limitations in GRIID research. However, across the GRIID domains, from realization of consciousness from unconsciousness to socio-psychological aspects of indigenous studies, and from examination of identity with a setting to its temporal and spatial changes, deductive reasoning cannot be applied universally; thus, the quantitative method faces limitations in addressing those issues.

Mixed method appropriateness

The appropriateness of mixed method depends on its transformative capacity, relating its axiom, ontology, and epistemology moving from obscurity to understanding that requires testing for casualty (Mertens, 2010).

Although some domains of GRIID research such as clinical case studies require both inductive and deductive, where knowledge can be built from the ground up based on observations through inductive reasoning and then verifying the theory construct through deductive reasoning (Southern & Devlin, 2010), in many cases the research can select one or the other. The combination of inductive and deductive reasoning can be used in GRIID domains such as evaluating justice or the level of injustice as perceived by the third parties in individual, social relationships and interactions, as long as an adequate frame of reference exists between the researcher and the subject in examining the topic and temporality is not an issue (Colquitt et al., 2015).

Summary

Research design is a function of the wording in the problem statement. When formulating a GRIID problem statement, the researcher should carefully select the wording to concisely explain the problem as indicated by a gap in literature, organizational, community, or individual issues, or sought-after interventions for clinical solutions. This chapter examined the context within which the research should be situated and the mechanics of how a researcher determines whether to use qualitative, quantitative, or mixed methods when conducting GRIID studies, along with examples.

EXERCISES

a   Examine the wording in your problem statement and focus on the specific problem and the research purpose. Based on the wording, how would you frame the study? Why? Explain.

b   Based on the framing from the first question, which method would you select? What sub-category within the method would you select? Why? Explain.

References

Ameel, E., Verschueren, N., & Schaeken, W. (2007). The relevance of selecting what's relevant: A dual process approach to transitive reasoning with spatial relations. *Thinking & Reasoning*, 13(2), 164–187. doi:10.1080/13546780600780671

Berger, R. (2015). Now I see it, now I don't: researcher's position and reflexivity in qualitative research. *Qualitative Research*, 15(2), 219–234. doi:10.1177/1468794112468475

Bhattacharya, K. (2007). Consenting to the consent form: what are fixed and fluid understandings between the researcher and the researched? *Qualitative Inquiry*, 13(8), 1095–1115.

Bickman, L., & Rog, D. J. (1998). *Handbook of Applied Social Research Methods*. Thousand Oaks, CA: SAGE Publications.

Bickman, L., Rog, D. J., & Hedrick, T. E. (2003). Applied Research Design: A Practical Approach. In L. Bickman & D. J. Rog (Eds.), *Handbook of Applied Social Research Methods* (pp. 5–37). Thousand Oaks. CA: SAGE Publications.

Bloor, M., Sampson, H., Baker, S., & Dahlgren, K. (2015). Useful but no oracle: Reflections on the use of a Delphi group in a multi-methods policy research study. *Qualitative Research*, 15(1), 57–70. doi:10.1177/1468794113504103

Brady, S. R. (2015). Utilizing and Adapting the Delphi Method for Use in Qualitative Research. *International Journal of Qualitative Methods*, 14(5), 1–6. doi:10.1177/1609406915621381

Bryman, A. (2006). Paradigm Peace and the Implications for Quality. *International Journal of Social Research Methodology*, 9(2), 111–126. doi:10.1080/13645570600595280

Buchanan, D., & Bryman, A. (2007). Contextualizing methods choice in organizational research. *Organizational Research Methods*, 10(3), 483–501.

Buckley, P., Chapman, M., Clegg, J., & Gajewska-De Mattos, H. (2014). A Linguistic and Philosophical Analysis of Emic and Etic and their Use in International Business Research. *Management International Review (MIR)*, 54(3), 307–324. doi:10.1007/s11575-013-0193-0

Cevolani, G. (2013). Truth approximation via abductive belief change. *Logic Journal of the IGPL*, 21(6), 999–1016.

Chiao, J. Y., Harada, T., Komeda, H., Li, Z., Mano, Y., Saito, D., Parrish, T. B., Sadato, N., & Iidaka, T. (2010). Dynamic cultural influences on neural representations of the self. *Journal of Cognitive Neuroscience*, 22(1), 1–11. doi:10.1162/jocn.2009.21192

Colquitt, J. A., Long, D. M., Rodell, J. B., & Halvorsen-Ganepola, M. K. (2015). Adding the 'in' to justice: A qualitative and quantitative investigation of the differential effects of justice rule adherence and violation. *Journal of Applied Psychology*, 100(2), 278–294.

Creswell, J. W. (2014). *Research Design: Qualitative, Quantitative, and Mixed Methods Approaches* (4th ed.). Thousand Oaks, CA: SAGE Publications.

Crow, G. (2000). Developing sociological arguments through community studies. *International Journal of Social Research Methodology*, 3(3), 173–187.

de Vries, P. H. (2004). Effects of binding in the identification of objects. *Psychological Research*, 69(1–2), 41–66.

Devine-Wright, P., & Clayton, S. (2010). Introduction to the special issue: Place, identity and environmental behaviour. *Journal of Environmental Psychology*, 30(3), 267–270. doi:10.1016/S0272-4944(10)00078-2.

Eckensberger, L. H. (2015). Integrating the Emic (Indigenous) with the Etic (Universal)-A Case of Squaring the Circle or for Adopting a Culture Inclusive Action Theory Perspective. *Journal for the Theory of Social Behaviour*, 45(1), 108–140. doi:10.1111/jtsb.12057

Fielding, N. (2014). Qualitative Research and Our Digital Futures. *Qualitative Inquiry*, 20(9), 1064–1073.

Gentsch, A., Weber, A., Synofzik, M., Vosgerau, G., & Schütz-Bosbach, S. (2016). Towards a common framework of grounded action cognition: Relating motor control, perception and cognition. *Cognition*, 146, 81–89. doi:10.1016/j.cognition.2015.09.010

Gross, J. J. (2002). Emotion regulation: Affective, cognitive, and social consequences. *Psychophysiology*, 39(3), 281–291. doi:10.1017.S0048577201393198

Haig, B. D. (2008). Précis of 'an abductive theory of scientific method'. *Journal of Clinical Psychology*, 64(9), 1019–1022. doi:10.1002/jclp.20506

Hall, S. M. (2013). The politics of belonging. *Identities*, 20(1), 46–53. doi:10.1080/1070289X.2012.752371

Harrison, D. A., & Klein, K. J. (2007). What's the difference? Diversity constructs as separation, variety, or disparity in organizations. *Academy of Management Review*, 32(4), 1199–1228.

Hughes, M. A., Price, R. L., & Marrs, D. W. (1986). Linking theory construction and theory testing: models with multiple indicators of latent variables. *Academy of Management Review*, 11(1), 128–144.

Hurdley, R., & Dicks, B. (2011). In-between practice: working in the 'thirdspace' of sensory and multimodal methodology. *Qualitative Research*, 11(3), 277–292.

Kilduff, M., Tsai, W., & Hanke, R. (2006). A Paradigm Too Far? A Dynamic Stability Reconsideration of the Social Network Research Program. *Academy of Management Review*, 31(4), 1031–1048. doi:10.5465/AMR.2006.22528168

Koro-Ljungberg, M. (2010). Validity, Responsibility, and Aporia. *Qualitative Inquiry*, 16(8), 603–610.

Lavallée, L. F. (2009). Practical Application of an Indigenous Research Framework and Two Qualitative Indigenous Research Methods: Sharing Circles and Anishnaabe Symbol-Based Reflection. *International Journal of Qualitative Methods*, 8(1), 21–40.

Liebig, S., Sauer, C., & Friedhoff, S. (2015). Using Factorial Surveys to Study Justice Perceptions: Five Methodological Problems of Attitudinal Justice Research. *Social Justice Research*, 28(4), 415–434. doi:10.1007/s11211-015-0256-4

Lincoln, Y. S., & Guba, E. G. (1985). *Naturalistic Inquiry*. Beverly Hills, CA: SAGE Publications.

Lycke, H. (2012). A formal explication of the search for explanations: the adaptive logics approach to abductive reasoning. *Logic Journal of the IGPL*, 20(2), 497–516.

Lynham, S. A. (2002). Quantitative Research and Theory Building: Dubin's Method. *Advances in Developing Human Resources*, 4(3), 242–276. doi:10.1177/15222302004003003

Maxwell, J. A. (1996). *Qualitative Research Design: An Interactive Approach*. Thousand Oaks, CA: SAGE Publications.

Maxwell, J. A. (1998). Designing a Qualitative Study. In L. Bickman & D. J. Rog (Eds.), *Handbook of Applied Social Research Methods* (pp. 69–99). Thousand Oaks, CA: SAGE Publications.

Mertens, D. M. (2010). Transformative Mixed Methods Research. *Qualitative Inquiry*, 16(6), 469–474.

Nicholls, R. (2009). Research and Indigenous participation: Critical reflexive methods. *International Journal of Social Research Methodology: Theory & Practice*, 12(2), 117–126. doi:10.1080/13645570902727698

Ong, B. K. (2012). Grounded Theory Method (GTM) and the Abductive Research Strategy (ARS): A critical analysis of their differences. *International Journal of Social Research Methodology*, 15(5), 417–432. doi:10.1080/13645579.2011.607003

O'Reilly, J., Aquino, K., & Skarlicki, D. (2016). The lives of others: Third parties' responses to others' injustice. *Journal of Applied Psychology*, 101(2), 171–189. doi:10.1037/apl0000040

Paternostro, D. C., & Marcotte, D. (2011). The story of the person: Integrating personalist philosophy with narrative psychology. *The Humanistic Psychologist*, 39(1), 24–36. doi:10.1080/08873267.2011.541371

Patton, M. Q. (2015). *Qualitative Research and Evaluation Methods: Integrating Theory and Practice* (4th ed.). Thousand Oaks, CA: SAGE Publications.

Pieterse, V., & Kourie, D. G. (2014). Lists, Taxonomies, Lattices, Thesauri and Ontologies: Paving a Pathway through a Terminological Jungle. *Knowledge Organization*, 41(3), 217–229.

Plato. (2017). *Allegory of the Cave*. Lulu.com.

Rabagliati, H., Doumas, L. A., & Bemis, D. K. (2017). Representing composed meanings through temporal binding. *Cognition*, 162, 61–72. doi:10.1016/j.cognition.2017.01. doi:013

Razack, N. (2005). 'Bodies on the move': spatialized locations, identities, and nationality in international work. *Social Justice*, 32(4), 87–104.

Reynolds, P. D. (1986). *A Primer in Theory Construction*. New York: Macmillan.

Sanders, P. (1982). Phenomenology: A New Way of Viewing Organizational Research. *Academy of Management Review*, 7(3), 353–360.

Soler-Toscano, F., Fernández-Duque, D., & Nepomuceno-Fernández, Á. (2012). A modal framework for modelling abductive reasoning. *Logic Journal of the IGPL*, 20(2), 438–444.

Southern, S., & Devlin, J. (2010). Theory Development: A Bridge between Practice and Research. *Family Journal*, 18(1), 84–87. doi:10.1177/1066480709358422

Strickland, B. (2017). Language Reflects "Core" Cognition: A New Theory about the Origin of Cross-Linguistic Regularities. *Cognitive Science*, 41(1), 70–101. doi:10.1111/cogs.12332

Tai, J., & Ajjawi, R. (2016). Undertaking and reporting qualitative research. *The Clinical Teacher*, 13(3), 175–182. doi:10.1111/tct.12552

Turri, J. (2014). *Epistemology: A Guide*. Hoboken, NJ: Wiley.

Wahyuni, D. (2012). The Research Design Maze: Understanding Paradigms, Cases, Methods and Methodologies. *Journal of Applied Management Accounting Research*, 10(1), 69–80.

Weiss-Cohen, L., Konstantinidis, E., Speekenbrink, M., & Harvey, N. (2018). Task complexity moderates the influence of descriptions in decisions from experience. *Cognition*, 170, 209 227. doi:10.1016/j.cognition.2017.10.doi:005

6

EXAMPLE, LESSONS, AND PITFALLS

When conducting research in gender, race, identity, indigeneity, and diversity (GRIID), as we explained in Chapter 1, researchers must clearly delineate the framework for the study and define the terms for the reader to discern the researcher's ontological and epistemological position for the research process to arrive at the results. We recommend examining the work of Creswell (2014), Huff (2009), or Patton (2015), who explain the required formatting for components of research such as the role and function of the abstract, introduction, background to the problem, problem statement, research question, the purpose of the study, the nature, operational definitions, its significance, and how the sections should be aligned. In this chapter, we will focus on the unique challenges of articulating GRIID studies.

GRIID research, like any other study, can follow the path for addressing a gap in the literature, searching for a solution to a practical problem, or clinical interventions to improve a process. However, the fundamental difference with other research is that any part of the GRIID research depends on the way humans formulate their thinking and manifesting them in some form of action, relations, or associations. Therefore, while following the same research process as other topics, starting with the background to the study, we will make a few suggestions and point out a few pitfalls. We conducted actual research on the question of social identity. Below we will share a few elements of the research that we used and ask you to fill in the other components and think about other ways of conducting the same research. Within each section, we (a) provide what we stated for our example research, (b) offer the items that you should be thinking about, and (c) describe the pitfalls that you should avoid.

PROBLEM STATEMENT: THE SPECIFIC PROBLEM IS HOW INDIVIDUALS PERCEIVE THEIR IDENTITIES.

Your task

- Starting with the identity definitions provided in Chapter 1, what should have been the preceding **introduction, background to the problem, the hook and anchor**, and **general problem**?

The pitfalls to avoid

- As you formulate your problem statement, think about your discipline and domain of inquiry. Also think about the setting. For example, is the problem focused on the social context of the identity or clinical? In addition, think about the differences in setting and the nature of participants and your expertise or lack of it in that setting. For instance, if you are examining identity based on how indigenous people perceive themselves within a country that has been occupied by colonists, then examine the effects of your ontology and your immediacy of understanding the nature of the indigeneity under consideration. In addition, think about how your investigative approach may not be suitable for obtaining objective results.
- When conducting research for a doctorate in philosophy, the problem statement must be rooted in the literature review; when conducting a DBA, clinical intervention, the problem statement must be based on a practical issue requiring resolution.

a Do not decide on a method before arriving at a concise problem statement. The wording in the problem statement would determine the appropriate method.

b Think about the originality of the research and its contribution to GRIID knowledge before formulating the problem statement.

c Think about the adequacy of participants' knowledge, etymology of language used to describe the problem statement to avoid issues in aligning the problem statement with other components of the study. For example, if you are examining the identity or any other problem related to Jingpo people in Myanmar, think about the way this particular group of people can best help you achieve new understanding; you should analyze and reflect on the qualitive or quantitative nature of the problem statement and its impact on the creation of new meaningful knowledge.

Purpose Statement: The purpose of this descriptive phenomenological research using Van Kaam's seven-step model as recommended by Moustakas (1994) was to use a semistructured interview method to describe the individuals' self-perception of identity…

Your task

- How did the purpose statement explain the method based on the specific problem statement? What key word in the problem statement inferred the purpose statement?

The pitfalls to avoid

- Selecting method before the problem statement will lead to confusing articulation of the purpose statement. If the purpose statement is more than half of one page, then more than likely you are adding elements that may not be relevant to the purpose, making the section wordy and unimpactful.

a Purpose statements in GRIID studies must be compatible with how the study intends to produce the results (Creswell, 2014). Therefore, the purpose must clearly be advantageous for creating the sought-after knowledge. In the purpose statement, the method design should reflect both the ontological position of the study and its epistemological underpinning. One should be mindful that in GRIID research the ontological lens (e.g., feminism and coloniality in examining women's role among Rakhine people in Myanmar) will impact the way a researcher arrives at new knowledge.

Nature of the study: The selected research method is a qualitative descriptive phenomenology.

...

Your task

- Explain the method that you will be using to conduct the research. Confine your explanation to less than three pages and avoid explaining why you would not use other methods in Chapter 1. Connect the nature to the problem statement and describe how your method will serve the purpose of the study. For example, when explaining the nature, the description should inform the reader why the method would serve to unearth the essence of the research question. Briefly explain how data is collected and analyzed in this section.

The pitfalls to avoid

- Selecting a method that cannot appropriately contextualize the GRIID topic within the specified discipline and domain. For example, if the topic of the study is addressing psychological aspects of identity by members of a Swahili group, the method should consider the temporality, spatiality, and the researcher's expertise in analyzing the participants' information based on the literary work that can help overcome coloniality and East African prevailing culture vis-à-vis the Swahili culture.

Research question/hypothesis: How do individuals perceive their social identity?

Your task

- Explain why this is a research question and why it does not allow for formulating hypotheses. Remember, the research focus and interest would be best served when there is one research question in the case of qualitative study and several hypotheses in quantitative studies, including a null hypothesis.

The pitfalls to avoid

- Avoid confusing the research question with the interview questions in qualitative studies. The purpose of interview questions is to answer the research question. Avoid adopting inappropriate method answering the research question. Here are some suggestions to help you navigate through the process:

a   Examine whether the problem statement wording indicates relationship between variables, requiring deductive reasoning, or infers an inductive approach. In the former case, quantitative study would be appropriate, requiring hypothesis testing based on the existing theories. In the latter case, the wording indicates that the problem poses a new area of inquiry without a *priori* knowledge about the problem.

b   Examine whether there is (a) adequacy of knowledge about the problem in a particular region, (b) a developed field of study about the topic and (c) awareness of the nature of the study by participants, particularly in quantitative studies.

Interview questions should help answer the research question. Therefore, for the sample study, the interview questions were as follows:

- RQ 1: How would you describe your identity? Why?
- RQ 2: How would you describe your gender, race, ethnicity? Why?
- RQ 3: How do you think your self-perception about yourself and the perception of others about you as an individual is the same or different? Why?

Due to the semistructured nature of the interviews, each question was followed by more open-ended questions as appropriate to arrive at an accurate understanding.

Data collection tools: For our sample research, the method and researcher are the instruments used to collect the data that will address each research question.

Data points yielded (list which specific questions/variables/scales of the instrument will address each research question): In our example study, the researcher sought to unfold the meaning and the method guides the process of meaning creation.

Data source (list which persons/artifacts/records will provide the data): In our example study, the sources were the interviewees.

Your task

- Explain how the research question/hypotheses and interview questions or surveys could have been restated to address social justice while observant of ontological position such as coloniality or feminism approaches to better understand how individual social identity.

The pitfalls to avoid:

- GRIID research questions/hypotheses, by its nature, regardless of the domain of inquiry (e.g., psychology, diversity, indigeneity), should provide significance for positive social change. For example, the research questions should indicate how the result of the research would provide meaningful help for patients, dispense social justice for those who are marginalized, or help improve inequities. Social justice provides an objective view for GRIID research because it is not subject to political bargaining nor can it be used as a "calculus of social interest" (*Rawls, 2005*, p. 4). *Weitz (1993)* argued that Rawls's definition of social justice is inadequate, particularly as one realizes that social justice is the result of rationalization of the state of the society rather than what one faces. Therefore, social justice, as *Weitz (1993)* viewed it and we concur with her, is the existential projection of academic ideas rationalizing it in whatever form it is manifested. Thus, the GRIID researcher must be aware of the role she plays in creating and embodying social justice and making positive social change. The GRIID researcher, in addition to accurate narration of a story, should be immersed in the research situation to grasp the gravity of the reality as it is presented to explain the research outcome in addressing social justice. Hence, the GRIID researcher must (a) reconcile fairness and self-interest to objectively assess and evaluate the needs and input of the participants in a study; (b) be aware of the conceptual frame, the personal psychology, and one's social disposition that influence the reconciliation of fairness and self-interest; and (c) be cognizant that the reconciliation of fairness with self-interest is based on the relationship of the researcher as the observer, the allocator of meaning, and the rewardee making sense of the data presented by the study (van den Bos et al., 2015).

TABLE 6.1 Interviewees' Demographic Information Summary

Demographic Information	Country of Birth	Nation-ality	Religion	Gender	Age	Profession
Respondent 1	USA	USA	None	Female	60–70	Professor
Respondent 2	Mexico	US/CA	Atheist	Female	40–50	Professor
Respondent 3	USA	USA	Non-practicing Methodist	Female	40–50	Professor
Respondent 4	USA	USA	Non-denomina-tional Christian	Woman	30–40	Higher Education
Respondent 5	USA	USA	None	Woman	20–30	Graduate Student
Respondent 6	Malaysia	USA	Free Thinker	Female	50–60	Educator

Our research findings illustrated the complexities of individual identity based on a myriad of groups (i.e., indigenous tribes, nationality, race, ethnicity, color, and religious beliefs and their intersectional influences). As Table 6.1 illustrates, the range of informants was limited by nationality and citizenship yet offered multiple perspectives on how individuals view various components of GRIID. The views offered by informants provided a non-uniform response to the relevance of various GRIID components to identity. As Table 6.1 shows, the elements such as prevalent family, group, or network association influence self-described identity. The findings provide ample information for relating the acquired data to the discussions in this chapter, which we will address next. It is important to note that the discussions with the participants revealed ambiguous cultural spaces yet with more pronounced self-perceived identity based on connection to family. In addition, the participants' responses were congruent with other findings that offered identity as a phenomenon related to time, space, and social relationships without fitting within a specific diversity category (Holck, Muhr, & Villesèche, 2016). For example, Informants 1 and 2 described their identities as *physical, mental,* and *learning from family through time.* In addition, dramatic changes such as immigration manifests profound effects.

As Table 6.2 outlines, some interesting facts emerged from the interviews about identity and its relation to gender, race, ethnicity, indigeneity, and culture, which will be discussed toward the end of this chapter.

RESEARCH FINDINGS

As Table 6.1 reveals, while some participants identified themselves as females, others chose to declare themselves as women. Therefore, demographic information may provide clues to the thinking of participants. In our sample study, we could discern the information due to the nature of the interview, building the demographic information into the questioning. However, when one sends a survey to participants, gender, race, and ethnicity information is articulated and stated from the researcher's perspective without allowing the participants to state them from their own perspective, which oversimplifies categorization. Incorrect demographic categorization can lead to incorrect assumptions about responses; hence, the analysis may be incorrect or skewed. The demographic information and its utilization can be more challenging when a survey is administered through electronic means or by individuals who are recruited to go into the field. As Table 6.2 illustrated, a researcher can get a glimpse of how individuals form and perceive their social identity and the context in which they formulate it.

Your task

- Explain how and why this research could have been conducted using the quantitative method? Also explain how and why the quantitative method may have not been appropriate for examining indigenous and autochthonous issues?
- Explain whether the current number of participants was adequate in arriving at a saturation point for adequate information available to thoroughly analyze the findings? Why? Why not?
- Explain how defining psychological, cultural, and social factors would have changed the analysis and the findings?

The pitfalls to avoid:

- In qualitative research:

a When analyzing the raw data, personal perceptions, worldview, and interjections may skew the results.
b Lack of sufficient contextualization and comparison with the known research on the topic may end in ironic analysis and results.
c If the study involved observations and experiments, analysis and findings should explain the relevance of methodology in arriving at the findings thoroughly.

- In quantitative research:

a When discussing the findings, the nature of methodology, the sampling biases, descriptive, and inferential statistics must be fully explained and describe how the results tested the theories that was intended to do.

Scholarly advice to PhD students in GRIID

Five prominent scholars in GRIID consented to participate by providing their insights based on more than a century of aggregate experience in the field. We have drawn from their participation and insights in completing this book and will

TABLE 6.2 Role of Identity

Informants	Identity	Shaping Identity	Identity Shifting	Changing Identity	Culture Influence on Identity	Race & Ethnicity Influence
#1	I've had lots of experience and... When you think about your identity, you also have to think about how other people perceive you. I was perceived as being this person	Family	I respond different to the environments	I don't change who I am inside, but how I present myself changes	Living in multiple cultures simultaneously as presented through media and reality	It's based on wealth, income, and position status
#2	normally [my identity] it's the opposite of what I think other people expect me to be	All experiences	[Based on expectations]	my identity is in transition	[other cultures impact one's identity]	[people may initially perceive my identity based on their expectation of my race and ethnicity until they get to know me].
#3	to say that living, growing up has just time. do that thing over and over and over	I feel like just going through life has really shaped me	[Based on expectations]	[referring to the period's music, political, and social environment the interviewee noticed changed in own identity]	[Culture I feel what is my parents has passed on to me as my heritage]	Race gave me my voice... I view race as a social construct that was designed to do certain things to certain people.

Informants	Identity	Shaping Identity	Identity Shifting	Changing Identity	Culture Influence on Identity	Race & Ethnicity Influence
#4	describe myself as a Black woman, a mother, and I guess I do that because those are the boxes that I check	I've also been highly introspective my entire life also my parents	[My self-perception and the perception of others on me are based on the environment in which I operate changes]	based on experiences	[Throughout the interview, the interviewee connected culture to parental guidance]	I use the term "Black" because. being from New York, it is very diverse and there's a lot of different types of nationalities. It is race, but for me it's also my ethnicity.
#5	I know that there's some level of potential ability, something that's in there that I haven't accessed yet	my parents	[my identity shifts based on who I am with]	[I would say definitely identity has changed through time]	[referred to social construction without addressing culture]	I felt like I was always trying to mute my race because everybody else was talking about it.
#6	We're just beings and then we attach our relationships and give ourselves identity	My mom. I think her values system	I am, what I'm doing, and I assume an identity for that moment	it's just experiences, in interactions with individuals, and how your perception over those positions have changed	The fact that that's no true national culture, even that national culture	everyone interacts, but you still have your own identity

Source: Research conducted October–November 2017

include quotes as evidence of their experiences to assist doctoral students and novice scholars in GRIID research.

Pitfalls to be reckoned with

Functionalist and individual paradigms have dominated the field with less attention to structural approaches to diversity in the workplace as well as the intimate relationship between subjectivity and systems of domination—for example, patriarchy, racism, heterosexism, and colonialism (Stella Nkomo).

The GRIID field seems to be reaching theoretical saturation (Eddy Ng) as not much new is coming forward. This is supported by Jenny Hoobler, who stated that "inequity/discrimination against women has been approached from so many angles and theories that it's very hard to say something new that doesn't just turn out to be 'old wine in new bottles.'" Stella Nkomo adds that it might be time to relook the meaning of diversity:

> The pursuit of validating the business case for diversity has overshadowed attention to social justice and practices that sustain inequality. It may be time to rethink the very label of diversity. This umbrella concept for different categories of difference may have obscured deep investigation into specific types of exclusion. While the intent was understandable, a negative consequence of the label has been the assumption that everyone is different and that "deep level" diversity is more significant than so-called "surface level" diversity. Yet, today's context offers a powerful reminder that issues of racism, sexism and homophobia remain salient despite efforts at inclusion.

Rana Haq stated:

> [T]he biggest pitfall is the nature of the GRIID topic itself because one would hope that this stream of research would not be necessary anymore if everyone was treated with respect, dignity, equality and inclusion in this day and age. However, the unfortunate reality is that in 2018 we are still researching GRIID issues which continue to be denied and minimized, yet perpetuated and reinforced within the mainstream of most societies worldwide in various sinister ways.

According to Eddy Ng:

> [R]esearch on diversity and inclusion cannot be undertaken with a "one size fits all" approach. We tried and failed. The landscape for diversity and equality in North America is very different from the one in Europe, Asia, Africa, or South America. National contexts, culture, stage of economic development, and workforce priorities differ from country to country and from region to region. For example, multiculturalism policies work in Australia and Canada, but not so

much in Europe. It would be more fruitful to approach our work from a comparative perspective to aid in understanding why certain policies or practices work well in one country or context but not in another.

Getting access to organizations or individuals for research in GRIID is difficult. This has been alluded to by Rana Haq:

> [M]ost people and organizations do not want to be negatively labelled or investigated in GRIID research. Therefore, since the topic is highly sensitive, most organizations do not like to talk about it, particularly if they are lacking, and either become defensive, refuse access to data or require anonymity so that the company cannot be identified.

The acceptance of students and studies in GRIID often pose difficulty, as the domain is broad and challenging. Stella Nkomo also explains these challenges:

> Doctoral students and novice researchers face two significant challenges in conducting research in the field. First is the challenge of doing research in a field that is not linked to traditional fields in management and organization studies [MOS]. Diversity, despite its importance, remains marginalized as a discipline in the majority of business schools and faculties of economic and management science. Thus, doctoral students and novice researchers typically have to identify a main area of research in which to establish themselves as scholars (e.g., human resource management, strategy and organizational behavior) even if their major interest is in diversity. Very few positions advertise academic positions in diversity. The second challenge is getting grounded in the rather large body of research generated over the past several decades. One indication of the maturity of diversity scholarship is the availability of a number of reviews published on the field.

Gender studies in Africa for African women are difficult, as mentioned by Julia Thondhlana:

> [W]hat the current more Western literature or theory defines as gender inequalities/inequities may be considered a normal way to behave in Africa. In many cases women studying and lobbying around gender issues are treated with suspicion by both male and female colleagues and students. In fact, negative treatment by other women can be the most discomforting. The paucity of success stories, gender role models as well as gender based violations of women by other women may make it difficult for more women to come forward and agitate around gender rights.

Research in GRIID is often viewed as a specialized field and not regarded as mainstream by the general research community. Eddy Ng summarized this as:

> [R]esearch on diversity and inclusion are often regarded as "specialized" and "niche," which gives it less standing than mainstream work in management and organizational behavior. As a result, journals that specialize in equality, diversity and inclusion (EDI) also receive less attention and are cited less often. By extension, scholars that work in this field and publish in these journals are often seen as less influential or impactful.

Stella Nkomo says it is not so difficult to conduct GRIID research anymore; however, getting published is another challenge: "[G]etting it published in top journals, especially if a doctoral student or novice researcher wants to investigate under studied areas in diversity (e.g., racism, sexism, homophobia, and diversity issues that are non-USA centric)."

As researchers in GRIID we need to take cognizance of the above pitfalls and address them in our research by becoming more innovative and learn from fields other than psychology and sociology by expanding to "political science, public administration, social work, community development, and even geography to move our field forward" (Eddy Ng). We also need to have bigger sample groups with intersectional differentiation especially in women studies, as stated by Jenny Hoobler: "getting samples large enough to have enough women in each cell/condition to make meaningful intersectional comparisons, and ensuring that your theory can speak across various demographic combinations."

General lessons from existing scholars

Eddy Ng:

> Diversity and inclusion is a multidisciplinary field. There are tremendous opportunities for cross-disciplinary work with colleagues in political science, public administration, social work, education, counseling, and media studies. Learn what other fields are writing on and researching about on diversity and inequality.
>
> Researching and writing about diversity and inclusion can be personal, but don't abandon oneself in the name of scientific objectivity. We have multiple identities and these identities become salient in different situations. We need to be able to explore our identities and connect them with our work, whether it's drawing attention to a stigmatized identity or recognizing our privilege. Find methodologies, such as auto-ethnography, that allow us to express ourselves through our work.
>
> There is a tremendous supportive community of diversity and inclusion scholars. They are very willing to mentor and support junior faculty. Many are now campus leaders, officers in professional associations such as the Academy of Management and journal editors. Reach out to them.

TABLE 6.3 Suggested GRIID research areas

Eddy Ng	Jenny Hoobler	Juliet Thondhlana	Rana Haq	Stella Nkomo
Research is needed to better manage an intergenerational workforce, negotiate the old and new ways of doing things, and facilitating knowledge transfer from one generation to the next. As the workforce in many countries are aging, the ramifications of a population cliff (e.g., one child policy in China) are acute. Many countries will experience a shortage of skills and labor, leading to declining production capacity. With longer lifespan, erosion of financial security, older workers are also participating in the workforce longer. What are some of the ways we can encourage older workers to support them and extend the backend of their careers?	Intersectionality: You can lead the senior researchers in this regard. We need to have more comprehensive pictures of the multiple identities that workers carry with them in the workplace and how these combine to equal more and less power in the workplace, as well as boundary conditions for these relations. Social psychology is way ahead of management on this; that discipline can help us get there.	More studies on the historical intersection of patriarchal traditions in the African context. The role of women in gender role construction and perpetuation. African women in leadership in different contexts.	Research has documented that people are tired of hearing about GRIID and even named it as "Gender fatigue" (which can easily be replaced by any of the other GRIID dimensions)! People may be tired of reading and writing about it yet they are not tired of perpetuating the GRIID issues in organizations and in society. I believe that, unfortunately, there will always be the need for new areas and ideas in GRIID research because we are nowhere near finding resolutions for all the GRIID issues currently present in this world. Since this is an international struggle, GRIID scholars need to familiarize themselves with the diversity of GRIID issues worldwide and pursue those which they are passionate about and invested in as there is a huge need for contextualizing GRIID research and aligning the methodology, conceptual framework, and epistemologies as well as comparative studies of best practices and benchmarking.	Consider qualitative methods or indigenous methods, particularly in addressing underexplored topics. Strive for a theoretical contribution and not merely an empirical one. Draw ideas from other disciplines; read work in sociology (particularly the sociology of work), critical studies, race and ethnic studies, post-colonial studies, and feminist scholarship. New context, due to changes in the workplace, gives rise to scholarly interest in how organizations should manage an increasingly diverse workforce. The political, historical, cultural, and demographic context of nations shape issues of difference and representation. Continuing inequality in organizations suggests that effective solutions to "managing diversity" have yet to be identified. Do more research that seeks to demonstrate and understand intersectionality. At the same time, transnationalism suggests intersectional mobilities—that is, intersectional positions are not fixed but mobile.

The pronouncement of multiculturalism is dead and the rise of post-multiculturalism has morphed into strong nationalistic sentiments. This has also contributed to greater xenophobia and anti-immigrant sentiment sweeping across the world. Large-scale immigration and refugee displacement will continue as individuals are in search of economic opportunities, escaping armed conflicts, and avoiding environmental degradation and disasters.	Interventions: We know there's a problem, what we now need to know is how to solve it. Same thing for gender scholars. There's discrimination. Through your research, help us find solutions to level the playing field. Test theoretically underpinned interventions (experiments, quasi-experiments) to see what works.	Meanwhile, the traditional GRIID issues are getting more complex and need to be addressed at multiple levels of intersectionality for true sense-making and resolution finding. Yet the younger generation seems to think that they now live in an equalized world and that the women's movement is passed. Diversity has been watered down into everyone being diverse! Organizations are finding more "palatable" ways for doing diversity. What does all this mean for GRIID research?	Much more research is needed on the creation of the "other" based on historical analyses of the effects of Western colonialism and its continuing effects from a postcolonial lens. The manifestation of inequality in organizations today have a long historical path that has yet to be fully interrogated.

Source: Verbatim data scripts from online participation (Haq, Hoobler, Ng, Nkomo and Thondhlana, 2018)

Jenny Hoobler:

> If you love it, do research in this area. I was told during my doctoral program that I would be branded a trouble-maker (read: feminist!) and never get a job in a business school if I pursued gender research. So I listened and did my thesis on a different topic. That move probably set my career back a little because my "brand" then became that other topic for several years. Only 6 years or so into my academic career did I become brave enough to actually pursue my passion—gender research. So perhaps I spent time and energy on a topic I'm not 100% passionate about, and, my research brand isn't as clear as it could have been. Don't listen to the haters.
>
> You're entering a supportive niche area—the nicest journal article reviews I tend to get are from other gender scholars. But I do not mean that these reviews are less rigorous/less challenging!

Rana Haq:

> GRIID research is a passion and calling. I do it for the personal satisfaction of being part of the conversation and contributing to the collective efforts of bringing about diversity awareness, education and training for creating positive social change. It is also a very personal issue since I grew up in India experiencing a privileged status due to my fair complexion and did not personally identify with racial discrimination until I migrated to Canada and was shocked at being considered to be a "woman of color." That was the first "aha" moment for me! It was only then that I recognized my earlier privilege and understood the concept better. So a personal investment is key to GRIID research.
>
> To top that was my religious identity as a Muslim, who are now regularly bombarded with aggressively negative stereotyping in recent years ever since 9/11. That is not to say that I had never faced discrimination. As a child and girl, I faced societal discrimination the moment I was born in India. Fortunately for me, I was born after three sons and after my parents had prayed fervently for a girl child and happily distributed sweets to the neighborhood after my birth, much to the dismay of their friends and society. Celebrating the birth of a girl child was unheard of. What a blessing for me to be born to my loving parents! Every child deserves to be loved and valued for s/he grows up into an adult who loves and values others too. So this was lesson number two for me—understanding where others are coming from. A sense of power, entitlement, loss, fear, consciously or unconsciously leads people to behave in desperately defensive or aggressively offensive ways. GRIID research finds ways to explore, understand and resolve these issues.
>
> In my experience, GRIID is generally a highly sensitive topic where organizations are lacking in many ways yet unwilling to go public with their challenges.

But with increased globalization, workforce mobility, Muslim refugees, etc., there is continuing, if not increased, need for everyone to be more aware, trained, and skilled in addressing GRIID issues.

Stella Nkomo:

Today questions of diversity in the workplace are global and more complex. Despite the budding literature on intersectionality, most diversity research often fails to consider how categories of difference are inexorably linked. For example, we often study gender in isolation of other categories of difference. The subjects of our research do not have single identities but multiple identities that position them within particular locations in organizations depending on salient factors in the context.

Take a more expansive understanding of the origins of diversity and not simply attribute its emergence to labor market trends in the USA.

New GRIID research areas/ideas suggested by experienced scholars

Table 6.3 includes the suggested areas of research in GRIID as proposed by experienced scholars.

Summary

This chapter provided examples of formulating components of a research proposal, explained the lessons based on the example provided, showed the creation of alignment between its components, and showed the pitfalls to avoid.

EXERCISE

Think about your degree program (whether practically or theoretically based) and state a concise problem statement. Based on the problem statement, write the purpose statement, research question/hypothesis, the nature of the study, the significance (including its positive social outcome), making sure the wording provides alignment among the components.

References

Creswell, J. W. (2014). *Research Design: Qualitative, Quantitative, and Mixed Methods Approaches* (4th ed.). Thousand Oaks, CA: SAGE Publications.

Holck, L., Muhr, S. L., & Villesèche, F. (2016). Identity, diversity and diversity management. *Equality, Diversity & Inclusion*, 35(1), 48–64. doi:10.1108/EDI-08-2014-0061

Huff, A. S. (2009). *Designing Research for Publication*. Thousand Oaks, CA: SAGE Publications.

Moustakas, C. E. (1994). *Phenomenological Research Methods*. Thousand Oaks, CA: SAGE Publications.

Patton, M. Q. (2015). *Qualitative Research and Evaluation Methods: Integrating Theory and Practice* (4th ed.). Thousand Oaks, CA: SAGE Publications.

Rawls, J. (2005). *A Theory of Justice* (Original ed.). Cambridge, MA: Belknap Press.

van den Bos, K., Cropanzano, R., Kirk, J., Jasso, G., & Okimoto, T. G. (2015). Expanding the horizons of social justice research: Three essays on justice theory. *Social Justice Research*, 28(2), 229–246. doi:10.1007/s11211-015-0237-7

Weitz, B. A. (1993). Equality and justice in education: Dewey and Rawls. *Human Studies*, 16(4), 421–434.

INDEX